Thanks for
your extraordniay
kidness —

I now
'intrigned' 'enlight
. end!

In

The Life of Thomas Chatterton, With Criticism on His Genius and Writings, and a Concise View of the Controversy Concerning Rowley's Poems

Never
forgotten,
J.R.
to R.C.
+

relation
to Keats,
I have
discovered
some powerful
parallels —
modernistic
phrases, as
well as a
deep love
for the poets
of English
language and
history

4/3/2017
Letter VIII in
appendix has a touch
of Keats' last letter —
the word 'adieu', and brave facade.

THE
LIFE
OF
THOMAS CHATTERTON,

WITH

CRITICISMS

ON HIS

GENIUS AND WRITINGS,

AND

A CONCISE VIEW

OF THE

CONTROVERSY

CONCERNING

ROWLEY's POEMS.

By G. GREGORY, D.D. F.A.S.

AUTHOR OF ESSAYS HISTORICAL AND MORAL, &c.

Agora com pobreza aborrecida,
Por hofpicios alheos degradado;
Agora da efperança ja adquirida,
De novo mais que nunca derribado.

CAMOENS.

LONDON.

PRINTED FOR G. KEARSLEY, No. 46, FLEET STREET.

1789.

[Price Five Shillings fewed.]

TO THE RIGHT HON. THE

MARQUIS of LANSDOWN.

My Lord,

PERMIT me to introduce the unpatronifed CHATTERTON to the only ftatefman of our time who has manifefted a genuine zeal for the promotion of literature and fcience. Had the unfortunate fubject of thefe pages but known, or had he made himfelf known to your Lordfhip, there is much probability that the world would at this day have continued to enjoy the increafing fruits of his uncommon talents.

It would, however, be the extreme of injuftice to confine your Lordfhip's commendation to the exercife of private munificence, or the admiration of learning. As one of that public, therefore, who are probably indebted for every thing which they poffefs or enjoy, to the

wifdom

wifdom and virtue of your Lordfhip's admi-
niftration, allow me to unite with all the ho-
neft and difcerning part of the community, in
expreffing my gratitude for the moft honourable and advantageous Peace which was ever
atchieved by this nation. When the little
contentions of Party are no more, and the
clouds of Faction are diffipated, the Friend of
Mankind and his Country will ftand confe-
crated to the veneration of pofterity; and it
will appear greater to have performed much
within a fhort period, than to have enjoyed
the emoluments of office for an age of inac-
tivity.

I have the honour to be,

MY LORD,

With great refpect,

Your Lordfhip's obliged

And faithful Servant,

Winkworth Buildings,
May 20, 1789.

The Author.

ADVERTISEMENT.

THE following pages were compofed at the requeft of the refpectable Editor of the Biographia Britannica, in order to be inferted in that valuable work. The author, however, requefted leave to print off a fmall edition, in a feparate ftate, for the accommodation and fatisfaction of a few friends, to whom he was indebted on the occafion for fome valuable communications.

Perhaps the admirers of CHATTERTON, and thofe in particular who have interefted themfelves in the controverfy relating to Rowley's Poems, will not be difpleafed at feeing collected in one view all the particulars which are known concerning that extraordinary character.

The only claim to the public approbation, which the author prefumes to affert in favour of this little volume, is that of authenticity, as the public may reft affured that no fact has been admitted but upon the moft unexceptionable teftimony. He is not at liberty to publifh all his authorities, but whenever they are known he is confident in the affertion, that they will be found highly refpectable. The notes marked O. were added by a moft learned and intelligent friend, who honoured the manufcript with his perufal.

THE
LIFE
OF
THOMAS CHATTERTON.

THE anceſtry of men of genius is ſeldom of much importance to the public or
their biographers; the commonwealth of
literature is almoſt a perfect democracy,
in which the riſe or promotion of individuals is generally the conſequence
of their reſpective merits. The family
of Chatterton, however, though in no
reſpect illuſtrious, is more nearly connected with ſome of the circumſtances
of his literary hiſtory than that of moſt
other votaries of the Muſes.—It appears
that the office of ſexton of St. Mary

Redcliffe

Redcliffe, in Briſtol, had continued in different branches of this family for more than one hundred and fifty years; and that John Chatterton, the laſt of the name who enjoyed that office, was elected in March 1725, and continued ſexton till his death, which happened in the year 1748[*]. Thomas Chatterton, the nephew of the preceding, and father to the extraordinary perſon who is the ſubject of theſe memoirs, had, we are informed, been in the early part of life in the ſtation of a writing uſher to a claſſical ſchool[†], was afterwards engaged as a ſinging man of the Cathedral of Briſtol, and latterly was maſter of the free ſchool in Pyle-ſtreet in the ſame city[‡]. He died in Auguſt 1752[||], leaving

* Dr. Milles's Preliminary Diſſertation to Rowley's Poems, page 6.

† Ibid.

‡ Ib. Mr. Bryant's Obſ. p. 514.

|| Ibid.

leaving his wife then pregnant of a son, who was born on the 20th of November, and baptized the 1ſt of January following, by the name of THOMAS, at St. Mary Redcliffe, by the Rev. Mr. Gibbs, vicar of that church.

The life of Chatterton, though ſhort, was eventful; it commenced as it ended, in indigence and misfortune. By the premature loſs of his father he was deprived of that careful attention which would probably have conducted his early years through all the difficulties that circumſtances or diſpoſition might oppoſe to the attainment of knowledge; and by the unpromiſing aſpect of his infant faculties he was excluded a ſeminary, which might have afforded advantages ſuperior to thoſe he afterwards enjoyed. His father had been ſucceeded in the ſchool at Pyle-ſtreet by a Mr. Love, and to his care Chatterton was committed at the age

of

of five years; but either his faculties were
not yet opened, or the waywardnefs of
genius, which will purfue only fuch objects as are felf-approved, incapacitated
him from receiving inftruction in the ordinary methods; and he was remanded
to his mother as a dull boy, and incapable
of improvement *. Nothing is more fal-
lacious than the judgments which are
formed during infancy of the future abilities of youth: Mrs. Chatterton was rendered extremely unhappy by the apparently
tardy underftanding of her fon, till *he fell
in love*, as fhe expreffed herfelf, with the
illuminated capitals of an old mufical manufcript, in French, which enabled her,
by taking advantage of the momentary
paffion, to initiate him in the alphabet †.
She taught him afterwards to read from an
old black-lettered Teftament, or Bible ‡.

Perhaps

* Bryant's Obfervations, p. 519.
† Ib. Milles's Prelim. Diff. p. 5.
‡ Milles's Prelim. Diff. p. 5.

Perhaps the bent of moſt men's ſtudies
may, in ſome meaſure, be determined by
accident, and frequently in very early life;
nor is it unreaſonable to ſuppoſe that his
peculiar attachment to antiquities may, in
a conſiderable degree, have reſulted from
this little circumſtance.

We are not informed by what means or
by what recommendation he gained ad-
miſſion into Colſton's charity-ſchool; but
doubtleſs, in the ſituation of his mother
at the time, it muſt have been a moſt de-
ſirable event; however unſuitable ſuch a
courſe of diſcipline might be to the improvement of Chatterton's peculiar talents.
Moſt of thoſe prodigies of genius, who
had hitherto aſtoniſhed mankind, by the
early diſplay of abilities and learning, had
been aided by the advantage of able in-
ſtructors, or had at leaſt been left at liberty
to purſue the impulſe of their ſuperior
underſtandings; it was the lot of Chatter-

B 3

ton

ton, to be confined to the mechanical drudgery of a charity-school; and the little ordinary portions of leisure, with which boys in his situation are indulged, was the only time allowed him to lay the foundation of that extensive and abstruse erudition which decorated even his early years. This seminary, founded by Edward Colston, Esq. is situate at St. Augustine's Back in Bristol, and is much upon the same plan with Christ's Hospital in London, (the only plan perhaps on which a charity-school can be generally useful,) the boys being *boarded* in the house, clothed, and taught reading, writing, and arithmetic. Chatterton, at this period, wanted a few months of eight years of age, being admitted on the 3d of August 1760*.

The

* On the authority of a letter signed G. B. dated Bristol, August 30, 1778, printed in the St. James's Chronicle. In Dr. Milles's Prelim. Diff. it is 1761; but this must be a misprint, as all agree that he was between seven and eight years old when admitted.

The rules of this institution are strict.
The school hours in summer are from
seven o'clock till twelve in the morning,
and from one till five in the afternoon; and
in winter, from eight to twelve, and from
one to four. The boys are obliged to be
in bed every night in the year at eight
o'clock, and are never permitted to be absent from school, except on Saturdays and
Saints days, and then only from between
one and two in the afternoon till between
seven and eight in the evening. The detail of these apparently trivial particulars
may at present favour of a culpable minute-
ness; but their importance will be experienced before I have concluded.

The first years of his residence at this
seminary passed without notice, and perhaps without effort. His sister, indeed,
in her letter to Mr. Croft, remarks, that
he very early discovered a thirst for pre-
eminence, and that even before he was

five years old he was accuſtomed to preſide
over his play-mates *. There is a curious
letter from Mr. Thiſtlethwaite of Briſtol,
publiſhed by Dr. Milles in his edition of
Rowley's Poems, which contains many
intereſting particulars concerning Chatterton. In the ſummer of 1763, Mr. Thiſtlethwaite, who was then very young, contracted an intimacy with one Thomas
Philips †, an uſher or aſſiſtant-maſter at
Colſton's ſchool. Though the education
of Philips had not been the moſt liberal,
he

* Love and Madneſs, p. 161. There is an anecdote of
Chatterton (it is given, however, only on a vague and in-
diſtinct report) partly to the ſame purpoſe. When very
young, a manufacturer promiſed to make Mrs. Chatterton's
children a preſent of ſome earthen-ware; on aſking the boy
what device he would have painted on his—" Paint me
(ſaid he) an angel, with wings, and a trumpet, to trumpet
my name over the world."

† In all probability the perſon on whoſe death Chatterton
compoſed an Elegy. I wiſh we were poſſeſſed of more perfect memoirs of Philips. His taſte for poetry excited a ſimi-
lar flame in ſeveral young men, who made no mean figure
in the periodical publications of that day, in Chatterton,
Thiſtlethwaite, Cary, Fowler, and others.

he yet possessed a taste for history and poetry; and by his attempts in verse, excited a degree of literary emulation among the elder boys. It is very remarkable, that Chatterton is said to have appeared altogether as an idle spectator of these poetical contests; he simply contented himself with the sports and pastimes which appeared more immediately adapted to his age; he apparently possessed neither inclination nor ability for literary pursuits, nor does Mr. Thistlethwaite believe that he attempted a single couplet during the first three years of his acquaintance with him*. Whatever grounds Mr. Thistlethwaite might have for this opinion, it, however, only serves to furnish an additional proof of the deceitfulness of those conjectures which are formed concerning the abilities of youth. The pert and forward boy, of active, but

superficial

* Milles's Rowley, p. 454.

fuperficial talents, generally bears away the palm from the modefty and penfivenefs of genius. Such a difpofition, which is in reality the refult of infenfibility, too frequently meets with encouragement, which produces indolence, impudence, and diffipation; while the lefs fhewy, but more excellent underftandings, are depreffed by neglect, or difheartened by difcouragement. Chatterton, doubtlefs, at that very period, was poffeffed of a vigour of underftanding, of a quicknefs of penetration, a boldnefs of imagination, far fuperior to the talents of his companions. But that penetration itfelf led him, perhaps, to feel more ftrongly his own deficiences; thofe delicate, yet vivid feelings which ufually accompany real abilities, induced him to decline a conteft, in which there was a danger of experiencing the mortification of being inferior. If he produced any compofitions, his exquifite

taſte

taſte led him to ſuppreſs them. In the
mean time he was laying in ſtores of information, and improving both his imagination and his judgment. About his tenth
year he acquired a taſte for reading; and
out of the trifle, which was allowed him
by his mother for pocket-money, he began to hire books from a circulating library.
As his taſte was different from children
of his age, his diſpoſitions were alſo different. Inſtead of the thoughtleſs levity
of childhood, he poſſeſſed the gravity,
penſiveneſs, and melancholy of maturer
life. His ſpirits were uneven; he was
frequently ſo loſt in contemplation, that
for many days together he would ſay very
little, and apparently by conſtraint. His
intimates in the ſchool were few, and
thoſe of the moſt ſerious caſt. Between
his eleventh and twelfth year, he wrote a
Catalogue of the Books he had read, to
the number of ſeventy. It is rather un-

fortunate

fortunate that this Catalogue was not preferved; his fifter only informs us that they
principally confifted of hiftory and divinity *. At the hours allotted him for play,
he generally retired to read, and he was
particularly folicitous to borrow books †.
Though he does not appear to have manifefted any violent inclination to difplay his
abilities, yet we have undoubted proofs
that very early in life, he did not fail to
exercife himfelf in compofition. His
fifter having made him a prefent of a
pocket-book as a New-Year's gift, he returned it to her at the end of the year
filled with writing, chiefly poetry ‡. It
was probably from the remains of this
pocket-book, that the author of Love and
Madnefs tranfcribed a poem, which appears by the date (April 14th, 1764) to
have

---

* Mrs. Newton's Letter in Love and Madnefs.
† Dr. Milles's Prelim. Diff, page 5.
‡ Mrs. Newton's Letter.

have been written at the age of eleven years and a half*. This fact is certainly

a strong

* It may not be improper to produce this poem, not only as it is the earliest existing specimen of Chatterton's compositions, but also for the sake of some remarks, which will probably throw some light on the genius and character of its author.

APOSTATE WILL, by T. C.

In days of old, when Wesley's pow'r
Gather'd new strength by every hour;
Apostate Will just sunk in trade,
Resolv'd his bargain should be made;
Then strait to Wesley he repairs,
And puts on grave and solemn airs,
Then thus the pious man address'd,
Good Sir, I think your doctrine best,
Your servant will a Wesley be,
Therefore the principles teach me.
The preacher then instructions gave,
How he in this world should behave,
He hears, assents, and gives a nod,
Says every word's the word of God.
Then lifting his dissembling eyes,
How blessed is the sect he cries,
Nor Bingham, Young, nor Stillingfleet
Shall make me from this sect retreat.
He then his circumstance declar'd,
How hardly with him matters far'd,
Begg'd him next meeting for to make
A small collection for his sake;

The

a ſtrong contradiction to Mr. Thiſtlethwaite's aſſertion, yet perhaps it is not

on

The preacher ſaid, do not repine,
The whole collection ſhall be thine.
With looks demure and cringing bows,
About his buſineſs ſtrait he goes ;
His outward acts were grave and prim,
The Methodiſt appear'd in him ;
But, be his outward what it will,
His heart was an Apoſtate's ſtill ;
He'd oft profeſs an hallow'd flame,
And every where preach'd Weſley's name ;
He was a preacher and what not,
As long as money could be got ;
He'd oft profeſs with holy fire,
The labourer's worthy of his hire.

It happen'd once upon a time,
When all his works were in their prime,
A noble place appear'd in view,
Then——to the Methodiſts, adieu ;
A Methodiſt no more he'll be,
The Proteſtants ſerve beſt for *he* ;
Then to the curate ſtrait he ran,
And thus addreſs'd the rev'rend man ;
I was a Methodiſt, 'tis true,
With penitence I turn to you ;
O that it were your bounteous will
That I the vacant place might fill !
With juſtice I'd myſelf acquit,
Do every thing that's right and fit.

The

on the whole fo difficult to be reconciled
as may at firft be fufpected. In the regifters
of

    The curate ftraitway gave confent——
    To take the place he quickly went.
    Accordingly he took the place,
    And keeps it with diffembled grace.

April 14, 1764.

In the firft place, this poem fhews the early turn and
bent of his genius to fatire, which predominated throughout
his fhort life, and with which he began and ended his literary career. Not only his fchool-fellows and his inftructors
became the fubjects of it at this early period, but his acquaintance and his friends felt its force.

In the next place, it appears that he was then no ftranger
to the works of Bingham, Young, and Stillingfleet, which
were probably among the books of divinity that compofed
the lift of thofe he had read or confulted, as mentioned in
Mrs. Newton's Letter.

Laftly, let it be obferved, that the perfon he fatirizes
is fuppofed to have turned methodift for mercenary mo-
tives, and to have preached the gofpel merely to put
money in his purfe.—Now Mr. Thiftlethwaite, in his letter
to Dean Milles, after mentioning Chatterton's intentions
of leaving his mafter's fervice and going to London,
fays—" I interrogated him as to the objects of his views
and expectations, and what mode of life he intended to purfue on his arrival at London. The anfwer I received was a
memorable one: 'My firft attempt,' faid he, 'fhall be in the
literary way; the promifes I have received are fufficient to
difpel doubt; but fhould I, contrary to my expectations,
find

of the memory, a few months is but a
trifling anachronifm; befides, tho' Chatterton might compofe at that time, it
does not follow that he was under any neceffity of imparting his compofitions to
Mr. Thiftlethwaite or Mr. Philips; indeed, he was the lefs likely to make them
public, as they were of the fatirical kind,
and confequently, if difcovered, the boy
                                    might

---

find myfelf deceived, I will in that cafe turn Methodift
preacher: Credulity is as potent a deity as ever, and a new
feft may eafily be devifed," &c.——*Milles's Rowley,*
page 459.

Chatterton might in fome meafure have in view the character which he had before fo fuccefsfully depicted, when he
thus expreffed himfelf to Mr. Thiftlethwaite. As his genius
was verfatile, and his reading extenfive; it is poffible this
profeffion might not be without fome ferious foundation;
indeed, if we are to believe that the fragment of a fermon,
which he produced as Rowley's, was really his own compofition, certainly many a quack preacher fets out upon a
much flenderer ftock of divinity than Chatterton was mafter
of at that time. The imagination, however, forms many
fchemes which the heart wants fortitude to reduce to action;
and perhaps, after all, his declaration to Mr. T. might be
no more than a temporary piece of gaiety, and that he
might ftill, though releafed from religious fcruples, abhor
the difhonourable character of a hypocrite.

might be apprehenſive of expoſing himſelf to puniſhment.

At twelve years old he was confirmed by the Biſhop: His ſiſter adds, that he made very ſenſible and ſerious remarks on the awfulneſs of the ceremony, and on his own feelings preparatory to it *. Happy had it been for him if theſe ſentiments, ſo congenial to the amiable diſpoſitions of youth, had continued to influence his conduct during his maturer years. He ſoon after, during the week in which he was door-keeper, made ſome verſes on the laſt day, paraphraſed the ninth chapter of Job, and ſome chapters of Iſaiah. The bent of his genius, however, more ſtrongly inclined him to ſatire, of which he was tolerably laviſh on his ſchool-fellows, nor did the upper-maſter, Mr. Warner, eſcape the rod of his reprehenſion. The firſt

C   poetical

* Mrs. Newton's Letter.

poetical essays of most young authors are
in the pastoral style, when the imagination
is luxuriant, the hopes and contemplations
romantic, and when the mind is better
acquainted with the objects of nature and
of the sight than with any other; but
Chatterton, without the advantages of
education or encouragement, and, on these
accounts, diffident perhaps of his own
powers, wanted the stimulative of indignation to prompt him to action; and a
quickness of resentment appears through
life to have been one of his most distin-
guishing characteristics *. From what has
been related, it is probable that Chatterton was no great favourite with Mr. Warner; he, however, found a friend in the
under-

---

* A late French writer, in his Memoirs of the poet De
la Harpe, who had manifested a like turn for satire in his
early years, says—" La satyre est la premiere qualité qui se
develope ordinairement dans un jeune poete. Celui se
l'exerce d'une façon ridicule envers ses maitres & meme
envers M. Assalin."

under-mafter, Mr. Haynes, who conceived for him, I have been informed, a ftrong and affectionate attachment.

A very remarkable fact is recorded by Mr. Thiftlethwaite in the letter already quoted. " Going down Horfe-ftreet, near the fchool, one day," fays he, " I accidentally met with Chatterton. Entering into converfation with him, the fubject of which I do not now recollect, he informed me that he was in the poffeffion of certain old manufcripts, which had been found depofited in a cheft in Redcliffe church, and that he had lent fome or one of them to Philips. Within a day or two after this I faw Philips, and repeated to him the information I had received from Chatterton. Philips produced a manufcript on parchment or vellum, which I am confident was Elenoure and Juga *, a kind

C 2

* See Rowley's Poems, p. 19, third edition.

a kind of paſtoral eclogue, afterwards publiſhed in the Town and Country Magazine
for May 1769. The parchment or vellum appeared to have been cloſely pared
round the margin; for what purpoſe, or
by what accident, I know not, but the
words were evidently entire and unmuti-
lated. As the writing was yellow and
pale, manifeſtly (as I conceive) occaſioned
by age, and conſequently difficult to de-
cypher, Philips had with his pen traced
and gone over ſeveral of the lines, (which,
as far as my recollection ſerves, were
written in the manner of proſe, and without any regard to punctuation,) and by
that means laboured to attain the object of
his purſuit, an inveſtigation of their meaning. I endeavoured to aſſiſt him; but
from an almoſt total ignorance of the characters, manners, language, and orthography of the age in which the lines were
written, all our efforts were unprofitably

2   exerted;

exerted; and though we arrived at the explanation of, and connected many of the
words, still the fenfe was notoriously deficient *." If this narrative may be depended on, Chatterton had difcovered thefe
manufcripts before he was twelve-years of
age. It is, however, fcarcely confiftent
with other accounts, fince both Mrs.
Chatterton and her daughter feem to be of
opinion, that he knew nothing of the
parchments brought from Redcliffe church,
which were fuppofed to contain Rowley's
poems, till after he had left fchool †.

Under all the difadvantages of education,
the acquifitions of Chatterton were fur-
prifing. Befides the variety of reading
which he had gone through, the author of
Love and Madnefs remarks, he had fome

C 3 knowledge

---

* Milles's Rowley.

† Milles's Prelim. Diff. p. 5. There appears good reafon for fufpecting fome miftake in Mr. Thiftlethwaite's narrative, either as to the date, or fome other circumftance.

knowledge of mufic *.—Is it not probable
that a few of the rudiments of vocal mufic made a part of the education of a charity boy? He had alfo acquired a tafte
for drawing, which afterwards he greatly
improved; and the ufher of the fchool
afferted he had made a rapid progrefs in
arithmetic †. Soon after he left fchool,
he correfponded with a boy, who had been
his bed-fellow while at Colfton's, and was
bound apprentice to a merchant at New-
York ‡. Mrs. Newton fays, he read a
letter at home, which he wrote to this
friend; it confifted of a collection of all
the hard words in the Englifh language,
and he requefted his friend to anfwer it in
the

---

* Love and Madnefs, p. 167.

† Ibid. p. 161.

‡ At the defire of this friend, he wrote love verfes to be
tranfmitted to him, and exhibited as his own. It is remarkable, that when firft queftioned concerning the old
poems, he faid he was engaged to tranfcribe them for a
gentleman, who alfo employed him to write verfes on a
lady with whom he was in love.

the fame ftyle. An extraordinary effect of his difcovering an employment adapted to his genius is remarked in the fame letter. He had been gloomy from the time he began to learn, but it was obferved that he became more cheerful after he began to write poetry*.

On the 1ft of July 1767, he left the charity-fchool, and was bound apprentice to Mr. John Lambert, attorney, of Briftol, for feven years, to learn the art and myftery of a fcrivener. The apprentice fee was ten pounds; the mafter was to find him in meat, drink, lodging, and clothes; the mother in wafhing and mending. He flept in the fame room with the foot-boy, and went every morning at eight o'clock to the office, which was at fome diftance, and, except the ufual time for dinner, continued there till eight o'clock at night,

after

† Milles's Prelim. Diff. p. 5.

after which he was at liberty till ten; when he was always expected to be at home. Mr. Lambert affords the moſt honourable teſtimony in Chatterton's favour, with reſpect to the regularity of his attendance, as he never exceeded the limited hours but once, when he had leave to ſpend the evening with his mother and ſome friends *. His hours of leiſure alſo Mr. Lambert had no reaſon to ſuſpect were ſpent in improper company, but generally with his mother, Mr. Clayfield, Mr. Barrett, or Mr. Catcott. He never had occaſion to charge him with neglect of buſineſs, or any ill behaviour whatever. Once, and but once, he thought himſelf under the neceſſity of correcting him, and that was the pure effect of his diſpoſition for ſatire. A ſhort time after he was bound to Mr. Lambert, his old ſchoolmaſter received a very

---

* Mrs. Newton's Letter above quoted.

very abuſive anonymous letter, which he
ſuſpected came from Chatterton; and he
complained of it to his maſter, who
was ſoon convinced of the juſtice of the
complaint, not only from the hand-writing,
which was ill-diſguiſed *, but from the
letter being written on the ſame paper
with that which was uſed in the office. On
this occaſion Mr. Lambert corrected the
boy with a blow or two. He, however,
accuſes him of a ſullen and gloomy temper, which particularly diſplayed itſelf
among the ſervants †. Chatterton's ſuperior abilities, and ſuperior information,
with the pride which uſually accompanies
theſe qualities, doubtleſs rendered him an
unfit inhabitant of the kitchen, where his
ignorant

---

*. This circumſtance is not unworthy of notice. If Chat-
terton was really the forger of the MSS. attributed to
Rowley, how came he in this inſtance to be unable to diſ-
guiſe his own hand-writing?

† From the information of Mr. Lambert to a friend of
the author.

ignorant affociates would naturally be inclined to envy, and would affect to defpife
thofe accomplifhments, which he held in the
higheft eftimation; and even the familiarity of vulgar and illiterate perfons, muft undoubtedly be rather difgufting than agreeable to a mind like his.

Mr. Lambert's was a fituation not unfavourable to the cultivation of his genius.
Though much confined, he had much
leifure. His mafter's bufinefs confumed a
very fmall portion of his time; frequently, his fifter fays, it did not engage him
above two hours in a day *. While Mr.
Lambert was from home, and no particular bufinefs interfered, his ftated employment was to copy precedents; a book of
which, containing 344 large folio pages,
clofely written by Chatterton while he remained in the office, is, I believe, ftill
in the poffeffion of Mr. Lambert, as
well

* Mrs. Newton's Letter above quoted.

well as another of about 30 pages;
The office library contained nothing
but law books; except an old edition
of Cambden's Britannia. There is no
doubt, however, but Chatterton took
care amply to supply his mental wants
from his old acquaintance at the circulating libraries.

He had continued this course of life for
upwards of a year; not, however, without some symptoms of an aversion for his
profession, before he began to attract the
notice of the literary world. In the beginning of October 1768, the new bridge
at Briftol was finished; at that time there
appeared, in Farley's Briftol Journal, an
account of the ceremonies on opening the
old bridge, introduced by a letter to the
printer, intimating that "The following
description of *the Fryars first paffing over
the old bridge*, was taken from an ancient
manufcript," and figned "Dunhelmus Brif-
tolienſ-

tolienſis *." The paper, if it be allowed
to be the fabrication of modern times, de-
monſtrates ſtrong powers of invention, and
an uncommon knowledge of ancient cuſ-
toms.

---

 * " Deſcription of the Fryars paſſing over the Old Bridge,
"taken from an ancient manuſcript.

" On Fridaie was the time fixed for paſſing the new-
" brydge. Aboute the time of tollynge the tenth clocke,
" Maſter Greggoire Dalbenye mounted on a fergreyne
" horſe, informed Maſter Maier all thynges were pre-
" pared, when two Beadils went firſt ſtreying ſtre. Next
" came a manne dreſſed up as follows, hoſe of gootſkyne
" crinepart outwards, doublette & waiſcot, alſo over which
" a white robe without ſleeves, much like an albe but not
" ſo long, reachinge but to his hands. A girdle of azure
" over his left ſhoulder, rechede alſo to his hands on the
" right & doubled back to his left, bucklynge with a goulden
" buckle dangled to his knee, thereby repreſentinge a Saxon
" earlderman.

" In his hands he bare a ſhield, the maiſtre of Gille a
" Brogton, who painted the ſame, repreſenting Sainte
" Warburgh croſſing the foorde ; then a mickle ſtrong man
" in armour, carried a huge anlace, after whom came ſix
" claryons & ſix minſtrels, who ſong the ſong of Sainte
" Warburgh. Then came Maſter Maier mounted on a
" white horſe dight with ſable trappyngs wrought about by
" the Nunnes of Saint Kenna, with gould and Silver, his
" hayre braded with ribbons & a chaperon with the auntient
" armes of Briſtowe faſtened on his forehead. Maſter Mair
" bare in his hande a goulden rodde, & a congean ſquire
" bare

toms! So singular a memoir could not
fail to excite curiosity, and many persons
became anxious to see the original. The
printer, Mr. Farley, could give no account
of

" bare in his hande, his helmet waulkinge by the syde of
" the horse. Then came the earlderman & city broders,
" mounted on sabyell horses dyght with white trappyngs &
" plumes & scarlet caps & chaperons having thereon sable
" plumes; after them, the preests & frears, parish mendicant
" & secular, some syngynge Sainte Warburghs songe,
" others soundynge clarions thereto & others some citri-
" alles.
" In thilke manner reachynge the brydge the manne
" with the anlace stode on the fyrst top of a mounde, yreed
" in the midst of the brydge, than went up the manne
" with the sheelde, after him the minstrels & clarions;
" and then the preestes & freeres all in white albes,
" making a most goodly shewe, the maier & earldermen
" standinge rounde, they songe with the sound of claryons,
" the songe of Sainte Baldwyne, which being done, the
" manne on the top threw with great myght his anlace into
" the sea & the clarions sounded an auncient charge &
" forloyne. Then theie song again the song of Sainte
" Warburge, & proceeded up Xts hill to the crosse,
" where a Latin sermon was preached by Ralph de Blun-
" derville, & with sound of clarion theye againe want to the
" brydge and there dined, spendynge the rest of the daye
" in sports and plaies, the freers of Sainte Augustyne doing
" the play of the knights of Bristow meekynge a great fire
" at night on Kynslate hill."

of it, nor of the person who brought the
copy; but after much inquiry, it was difcovered that the manuscript was brought by
a youth between fifteen and sixteen years of
age, of the name of Thomas Chatterton *.
" To the threats of those who treated
him (agreeably to his appearance) as a
child, he returned nothing but haughti-
ness, and a refusal to give any account †."
By milder usage he was somewhat soften-
ed, and appeared inclined to give all the
information in his power. He at first alledged, that he was employed to transcribe
the contents of certain ancient manuscripts
by a gentleman, who also had engaged
him to furnish complimentary verses, in-
scribed to a lady with whom that gentleman was in love. On being further pressed,
he at last informed the inquirers, that he
had received the paper in question, together
with many other manuscripts, from his
father,

* Preface to Rowley's Poems.
† Croft's Love and Madness, p. 145.

father, who had found them in a large chest in the upper room over the chapel, on the north side of Redcliffe church *: But a still more circumstantial account of the discovery of these manuscripts, is preserved in Mr. Bryant's Observations on Rowley's Poems. Over the north porch of St. Mary Redcliffe church, which was founded, or at least rebuilt, by Mr. W. Canynge, (an eminent merchant of Bristol in the 15th century, and in the reign of Edward the Fourth,) there is a kind of muniment room, in which were deposited six or seven chests, one of which in particular was called *Mr. Canynge's cofre* †; this chest, it is said, was secured by six keys,

* See Mr. Catcott's account in the preface to Rowley's poems.

† When rents were received and kept in specie, it was usual for corporate bodies to keep the writings and rents of estates left for particular purposes, in chests appropriated to each particular benefaction, and called by the benefactor's name; several old chests of this kind are still existing in the University of Cambridge. O.

keys, two of which were entrusted to the
minister and procurator of the church; two
to the mayor, and one to each of the
church-wardens. In proceſs of time,
however, the ſix keys appear to have been
loſt; and about the year 1727, a notion
prevailed that ſome title deeds, and other
writings of value, were contained in Mr.
Canynge's cofre. In conſequence of this
opinion, an order of veſtry was made, that
the cheſt ſhould be opened under the in-
ſpection of an attorney; and that thoſe
writings, which appeared of conſequence,
ſhould be removed to the ſouth porch of
the church. The locks were therefore
forced, and not only the principal cheſt,
but the others, which were alſo ſuppoſed
to contain writings, were all broken open.
The deeds immediately relating to the
church were removed, and the other manuſcripts were left expoſed as of no value.
Conſiderable depredations had, from time

to time, been committed upon them, by different persons; but the most insatiate of these plunderers was the father of Chatterton. His uncle being sexton of St. Mary Redcliffe gave him free access to the church. He carried off, from time to time, parcels of the parchments, and one time alone, with the assistance of his boys, is known to have filled a large basket with them. They were deposited in a cupboard in the school, and employed for different purposes, such as the covering of copy books, &c.; in particular, Mr. Gibbs, the minister of the parish, having presented the boys with twenty bibles, Mr. Chatterton, in order to preserve these books from being damaged, covered them with some of the parchments. At his death, the widow being under a necessity of removing, carried the remainder of them to her own habitation. Of the discovery of their value by the younger Chatterton,

D the

the account of Mr. Smith, a very intimate
acquaintance, which he gave to Dr. Glynn
of Cambridge, is too interefting to be
omitted. " When young Chatterton was
firſt articled to Mr. Lambert, he uſed
frequently to come home to his mother,
by way of a fhort vifit. There, one day,
his eye was caught by one of thefe parchments, which had been converted into a
thread-paper. He found not only the
writing to be very old, the characters very
different from common characters, but
that the ſubject therein treated was different
from common ſubjects. Being naturally
of an inquifitive and curious turn, he was
very much ftruck with their appearance,
and, as might be expected, began to queftion his mother what thofe thread-papers
were, how fhe got them, and whence
they came. Upon farther enquiry, he was
led to a full difcovery of all the parchments

ments which remained * ;" the bulk of
them confifted of poetical and other compofitions, by Mr. Canynge, and a particular friend of his, Thomas Rowley, whom
Chatterton at firft called a monk, and afterwards a fecular prieft of the fifteenth
century. Such, at leaft, appears to be
the account which Chatterton thought
proper to give, and which he wifhed to be
believed. It is, indeed, confirmed by the
teftimony of his mother and fifter. Mrs.
Chatterton informed a friend of the Dean
of Exeter, that on her removal from
Pyle-ftreet, fhe emptied the cupboard of
its contents, partly into a large long deal
box, where her hufband ufed to keep his
clothes, and partly into a fquare oak box
of a fmaller fize ; carrying both with their
contents to her lodgings, where, according to her account, they continued neglected

D 2 and

* Bryant's Obfervations, p. 511—529.

and undisturbed, till her son first discovered their value; who having examined
their contents, told his mother, 'that he
had found a treasure, and was so glad
nothing could be like it.' That he then
removed all these parchments out of the
large long deal box, in which his father
used to keep his clothes, into the square
oak box: That he was perpetually ran-
sacking every corner of the house for more
parchments, and, from time to time, carried
away those he had already found by pockets
full: That one day happening to see
Clarke's History of the Bible covered with
one of those parchments, he swore a great
oath, and stripping the book, put the
cover into his pocket, and carried it away;
at the same time stripping a common little
Bible, but finding no writing upon the
cover, replaced it again very leisurely *.

                       " Upon

---

* Milles's Prelim. Diff p. 7. It does not appear that
any of the parchments exhibited to Mr. Barrett, or Mr.
Catcott.

"Upon being informed of the manner in which his father had procured the parchments, he went himself to the place, and picked up four more, which, if Mrs. Chatterton rightly remembers, Mr. Barrett has at this time in his possession *."

" Mrs. Newton, his sister, being asked, if she remembers his having mentioned Rowley's poems, after the discovery of the parchments; says, that he was perpetually talking on that subject, and once in particular, (about two years before he left Bristol) when a relation, one Mr. Stephens of Salisbury, made them a visit, he talked of nothing else.†."

Nearly about the time when the paper in Farley's Journal, concerning the old bridge, became the subject of conversation,

as

Catcott, were of a size sufficient for a covering for an octavo book; much less for a quarto or folio. O.

* Milles's Prelim. Diss. p. 7.

† Ibid.

as Mr. Catcott of Briftol, a gentleman of
an inquifitive turn, and fond of reading,
was walking with a friend in Redcliffe
church, he was informed by him of feveral ancient pieces of poetry, which had
been found there, and which were in the
poffeffion of a young perfon with whom he
was acquainted. This perfon proved to
be Chatterton, to whom Mr. Catcott de-
fired to be introduced. He accordingly
had an interview; and foon after, obtained
from him, very readily, without any reward, the Briftow Tragedy *, Rowley's
Epitaph upon Mr. Canynge's anceftor †,
with fome other fmaller pieces. In a few
days he brought fome more, among which
was *the Yellow Roll*. About this period,
Mr. Barrett, a refpectable furgeon in Briftol, and a man of letters, had projected a
hiftory of his native city, and was anxi-
ously

* See Rowley's Poems, p. 44.
† Ibid. p. 277.

oufly collecting materials for that work.
Such a difcovery, therefore, as that of
Chatterton, could fcarcely efcape the vigi-
lance of Mr. Barrett's friends. The pieces
in Mr. Catcott's poffeffion, of which fome
were copies and fome originals, were immediately communicated to Mr. Barrett,
whofe friendfhip and patronage by thefe
means our young literary adventurer was
fortunate enough to fecure. During the
firft converfations which Mr. Catcott had
with him, he heard him mention the
names of moft of the poems fince printed,
as being in his poffeffion. He afterwards
grew more fufpicious and referved; and it
was but rarely, and with difficulty, that
any more originals could be obtained
from him. He confeffed to Mr. Catcott
that he had deftroyed feveral; and fome
which he owned to have been in his poffeffion, were never afterwards feen. One
of thefe was the tragedy of the Apoftate,

of

of which a fmall part only has been preferved by Mr. Barrett. The fubject of it
was the apoftatizing of a perfon from the
Chriftian to the Jewifh faith *. Mr. Barrett, however, obtained from him at different times feveral fragments; fome of
them of a confiderable length; they are all
written upon vellum, and he afferted them
to be a part of the original manufcripts,
which he had obtained in the manner which
has been already related. A *fac fimile* of
one of thefe fragments is publifhed in
Mr. Tyrwhitt's and Dr. Milles's editions
of Rowley's Poems; and the fragments in
profe, which are confiderably larger, we
are taught to expect in Mr. Barrett's Hiftory of Briftol. In the fame work we are
alfo promifed " *A Difcorfe on Briftowe*,
and the other hiftorical pieces in profe,
which Chatterton at different times de-
livered

---

* Bryant's Obfervations, p. 517.

livered out, as copied from Rowley's manuscripts *."

The friendship of Mr. Barrett and Mr. Catcott was of considerable advantage to Chatterton. They supplied him occasionally with money, as a compensation for some of the fragments of Rowley, with which he gratified them †. He spent many agreeable hours in their company; and their acquaintance introduced him into a more respectable line than he could easily have attained without it. His sister remarks, that after he was introduced to these gentlemen, his ambition daily and perceptibly encreased; and he would frequently

---

* Preface to Rowley's Poems, p. 11. It is now said that Mr. B. does not mean to insert any of these pieces in his History.

† Some of his later compositions, however, demonstrate, that he was not thoroughly satisfied with his Bristol patrons; and Mr. Thistlethwaite does not hesitate to assert, that he felt himself greatly disappointed in his expectations of pecuniary rewards for his communications. K.

quently speak in raptures of the undoubted success of his plan for future life. " When in spirits, he would enjoy his rising fame, and, confident of advancement, he would promise his mother and I should be partakers of his succefs *. Both these gentlemen also lent him books; Mr. Barrett lent him several medical authors †, and, at his request, gave him some in-instructions in surgery. His taste was verfatile, and his studies various. In the course of the years 1768 and 1769, Mr. Thistlethwaite frequently saw him, and describes in a lively manner the employ-ment of his leisure hours. " One day," says Mr. T. " he might be found busily employed in the study of heraldry and English antiquities, both of which are numbered among the most favourite of his pursuits;

* Mrs. Newton's letter before quoted.

† Ibid.

pursuits; the next discovered him deeply
engaged, confounded and perplexed amidst
the subtleties of metaphysical disquisition,
or lost and bewildered in the abstruse
labyrinth of mathematical researches; and
these in an instant again neglected and
thrown aside, to make room for music
and astronomy, of both which sciences his
knowledge was entirely confined to theory.
Even physic was not without a charm to
allure his imagination, and he would talk
of Galen, Hippocrates, and Paracelsus,
with all the confidence and familiarity of a
modern empirick *." It may naturally be
supposed, that his acquaintance with most
of these sciences was very superficial; but
his knowledge of antiquities was extensive,
and we might perhaps say profound. With
a view of perfecting himself in these favourite studies, he borrowed Skinner's

Etymologicon

* Milles's Rowley, p. 456.

Etymologicon of Mr. Barrett, but returned it in a few days as useless, most of the
interpretations being in Latin. He also
borrowed Benson's Saxon Vocabulary, but
returned it immediately on the same account *. His disappointment was partly
compensated by the acquisition of Ker-
sey's Dictionary, and Speght's Chaucer,
(the Glossary to which he carefully
transcribed †.) With these books he
was furnished by Mr. Green, a bookseller in Bristol. Probably the mortification he received at not being able to
make that use which he desired of Skinner
and of Benson, might be an additional stimulative to the great inclination which
he manifested to acquaint himself with
Latin, and his design to attempt it without a master. From this project his friend,
Mr. Smith, took great pains to dissuade
him,

---

* Bryant's Observ. p. 532.
† Milles's Prelim. Diss. p. 5, and 17.

him, and advifed him rather to apply to French, a competent knowledge of which might be fooner attained, and which promifed to be of more effential fervice *. Whatever plan he adopted, he entered upon it with an earneftnefs and fervour almoft unexampled: Indeed, the poetic enthufiafm was never more ftrongly exhibited than in Chatterton. Like Milton, he fancied he was more capable of writing well at fome particular times than at others, and the full of the moon was the feafon when he imagined his genius to be in perfection; at which period, as if the immediate prefence of that luminary added to the infpiration, he frequently devoted a confiderable portion of the night to compofition †.—"He was always," fays Mr. Smith, "extremely fond of walking in the fields, particularly in Redcliffe meadows, and of talking about thefe

(Row-

* Bryant's Obferv. p. 532.
† Mrs. Newton's letter to Mr. C.

(Rowley's) manuscripts, and sometimes
reading them there. " Come (he would
" say) you and I will take a walk in the
" meadow. I have got the cleverest thing
" for you imaginable. It is worth half-
" a crown merely to have a sight of it,
" and to hear me read it to you." When
we arrived at the place proposed, he would
produce his parchment, shew it and read
it to me. There was one spot in particular, full in view of the church, in which
he seemed to take a peculiar delight. He
would frequently lay himself down, fix
his eyes upon the church, and seem as if
he were in a kind of trance. Then, on a
sudden and abruptly, he would tell me,
" that steeple was burnt down by light-
" ning: that was the place where they
" formerly acted plays *." His Sundays
were commonly spent in walking alone into the country about Bristol, as far as the

duration

---

* Bryant's Observ. p. 530.

duration of day-light would allow; and from these excursions he never failed to bring home with him drawings of churches, or of some other objects, which had impressed his romantic imagination *.

His attention, while at Bristol, was not confined to Rowley; his pen was exercised in a variety of pieces, chiefly satirical, and several essays, both in prose and verse, which he sent to the Magazines. I have not been able to trace any thing of Chatterton's in the Town and Country Magazine (with which he appears to have first corresponded) before February 1769; but in the acknowledgments to correspondents for November 1768, we find "D. B. of Bristol's favour will be gladly received."

Dunhelmus

* Love and Madness, p. 159. The Dean of Exeter mentions drawings by Rowley of Bristol Castle, which he supposes genuine, but which Mr. Warton reprobates as fictions of Chatterton, the representations of a building which never existed, in a capricious, affected style of Gothic architecture, reducible to no system. O.

Dunhelmus Briftolienfis was the signature he generally employed. In the course of the year 1769, he was a considerable contributor to that publication. One of the firſt of his pieces which appeared was a letter on the tinctures of the Saxon heralds, dated Briſtol, February 4; and in the fame Magazine a poem was inferted on Mr. Alcock, of Briſtol, an excellent miniature painter, ſigned *Afaphides* *. In the fame Magazine for March are ſome extracts from Rowley's manuſcripts; and in different numbers: for the ſucceeding months, ſome pieces called Saxon poems, written in the ſtyle of Oſſian.

The whole of Chatterton's life preſents a fund of uſeful inſtruction to young perſons of brilliant and lively talents, and affords a ſtrong diſſuaſive againſt that impetuoſity

---

* This piece, with two or three others in Chatterton's Miſcellanies, was claimed by John Lockſtone, a linendraper in Briſtol, a great friend of Chatterton; by his confeſſion, however, it was corrected by the latter.

petuolity of expectation, and those delu-
sive hopes of success, founded upon the
conscioufnefs of genius and merit, which
lead them to neglect the ordinary means of
acquiring competence and independence.
The early difguft which Chatterton conceived for his profeffion, may be accounted one of the prime fources of his misfortunes. Among the efforts which he made
to extricate himfelf from this irkfome fituation, the moft remarkable is his application
to the Hon. Horace Walpole, in March
1769 * ; the ground of which was an offer
to furnifh him with fome accounts of a
feries of great painters, who had flourifhed
at Briftol, which Chatterton faid had been
lately difcovered, with fome old poems,
in that city. The pacquet fent by Chatterton was left at Bathurft's, Mr. Walpole's bookfeller, and contained, befide

E this

* Two Letters by the Honourable Horace Walpole,
p. 55.

this letter, an ode or little poem, of two
or three ftanzas in alternate rhyme, on the
death of Richard I. as a fpecimen of the
poems which were found. Mr. Walpole had
but juft before been made the inftrument
of introducing into the world Mr. M'Pher-
fon's forgeries; a fimilar application, therefore, ferved at once to awaken his fufpi-
cion. He, however, anfwered Chatterton's letter, defiring further information;
and in reply, was informed, that "he,
(Chatterton) was the fon of a poor widow,
who fupported him with great difficulty;
that he was apprentice to an attorney, but
had a tafte for more elegant ftudies," The
letter hinted a wifh that Mr. Walpole
would affift him in emerging from fo dull
a profeffion, by procuring fome place, in
which he might purfue the natural bias
of his genius. He affirmed that great
treafures of ancient poetry had been difcovered at Briftol, and were in the hands
of a perfon who had lent him the fpecimen

men already tranfmitted, as well as a paftoral (Elinoure and Juga) which accompanied this fecond letter. Mr. Walpole
wrote to a friend, a noble lady at Bath,
to enquire after the author of thefe letters,
who found his account of himfelf verified
in every particular. In the mean time the
fpecimens were communicated to Mr.
Gray and Mr. Mafon, and thofe gentlemen, at firft fight, pronounced them
forgeries. Mr. Walpole, though convinced of the author's intention to impofe
upon him, could not, as he himfelf con-
feffes, help admiring the fpirit of poetry
which animated thefe compofitions. The
teftimonies of his approbation, however,
were too cold to produce in Chatterton
any thing but lafting difguft. Mr. Walpole's reply was indeed (according to his
own account) rather too much in the
common-place ftyle of Court replies;
though fome allowance is to be made for

E 2   his

his peculiar situation, and for his juft ap-
prehenfion of a new impofition to be prac-
tifed on him. He complained in general
terms of his want of power to be a patron,
and advifed the young man to apply himfelf to the duties of his profeffion, as more
certain means of attaining the independence
and leifure of which he was defirous.
This frigid reception extracted immediately from Chatterton, "a peevifh letter,"
defiring the manufcripts back, as they
were the property of another; and Mr.
Walpole, either offended at the warm and
independent fpirit which was manifefted
by the boy, or pleafed to be difengaged
from the bufinefs in fo eafy a manner,
proceeded on a journey to Paris, without
taking any further notice of him. On
his return, which was not for fome time,
he found another epiftle from Chatterton,
in a ftyle (as he terms it) "fingularly impertinent;" expreffive of much refent-
ment

ment on account of the detention of his poems, roughly demanding them back, and adding, " that Mr. Walpole would not have *dared* to use him so ill, had he not been acquainted with the narrowness of his circumstances." The consequence was, therefore, such as might be expected. Mr. Walpole returned his poems and his letters in a blank cover, and never afterwards heard from him or of him during his life *. The affront was never forgiven by the disappointed poet, though it is perhaps more than repaid by the ridiculous portrait which he has exhibited of Mr. W———; in the Memoirs of a Sad Dog, under the character of " the redoubted Baron Otranto †, who has spent his whole life in conjectures."

On the score of these transactions, Mr. Walpole has incurred more censure than he

E 3

* Ib. passim.
† Chat. Miscel. p. 184.

he really deserved. In an age when literature is so little patronized by those who
wield all the powers of the state, and have
in trust for the public the distribution of
its emoluments; when men of the first
abilities, actually engaged in the learned
professions, are permitted to languish in
obscurity and poverty, without any of those
rewards, which are *appropriated* to the
professions they exercise; and are compelled
to depend for a precarious subsistence on
the scanty pittance, which they derive
from diurnal drudgery in the service of
booksellers, it can scarcely be deemed an
instance of extraordinary illiberality that a
private man, though a man of fortune,
should be inattentive to the petition of a
perfect stranger, a young man, whose
birth or education entitled him to no high
pretensions, and who had only conceived
an unreasonable dislike to a profession both
lucrative and respectable. If Chatterton

had

had actually avowed the poems, perhaps a very generous and feeling heart, such as rarely exists at present, and least of all in the higher circles of life, might have been more strongly affected with their beauties, and might probably have extended some small degree of encouragement. But considering things as they are, and not as they ought to be, it was a degree of unusual condescension to take any notice whatever of the application; and when Chatterton felt so poignantly his disappointment, he only demonstrated his ignorance of the state of patronage in this country, and acted like a young and ingenuous person, who judged of the feelings of courtiers by the generous emotions of his own breast, or the practice of times, which exist now only in the records of romance. Mr. Walpole afterwards regretted, and I believe sincerely, that he had not seen this extraordinary youth, and that he did not pay a

E 4 more

more favourable attention to his correſpondence; but, to be neglected in life,
and regretted and admired when theſe
paſſions can be no longer of ſervice, has
been the uſual fate of learning and genius.
Mr. Walpole was certainly under no obligation of patronizing Chatterton. To
have encouraged and befriended him, would
have been an exertion of liberality and munificence uncommon in the preſent day;
but to aſcribe to Mr. Walpole's neglect
(if it can even merit ſo harſh an appella-
tion) the dreadful cataſtrophe, which happened at the diſtance of nearly two years
after, would be the higheſt degree of in-
juſtice and abſurdity *.

                                    The

---

* A learned and reſpectable friend, on reading theſe memoirs in manuſcript, favoured me with the following able
vindication of Mr. W. which, for the ſatisfaction of thoſe
who wiſh for the fulleſt information on the ſubject, I inſert
intire.

    It has already been ſtated, that, in March 1769, Chat-
terton, not long after his acquaintance with Mr. Barrett
                                              and

The reader has hitherto contemplated Chatterton in the pleasing light of an ingenious

and Mr. Catcott, to whom he had communicated some originals and some transcripts of Rowley's Poems, wrote a letter to Mr. H. Walpole, inclosing also a specimen of the poems, and soliciting his patronage. Let the reader take the account in Mr. Walpole's own words, from an extract of a letter to Mr. W. B. added to another letter to the Editor of Chatterton's Miscellanies, and printed at Strawberry-hill, 1779.

"I am far from determined to publish any thing about "Chatterton. It would almost look like making myself a "party. I do not love controversy; if I print, my chief "reason would be, that both in the account of the poems, "and in Mr. Warton's last volume, my name has been "brought in with so little circumspection and accuracy, "that it looks as if my rejection of Chatterton had driven "him to despair; whereas I was the first person on whom "he essayed his art and ambition, instead of being the "last. I never saw him; there was an interval of near two "years between his application to me and his dismal end; "nor had he quitted his master, nor was necessitous, nor "otherwise poor than attornies clerks usually are; nor had "he come to London, nor launched into dissipation, when "his correspondence with me stopped. As faithfully as I "can recollect the circumstances, without dates, and "without searching for what few memorandums I pre-"served relative to him, I will recapitulate his history "with me. Bathurst, my bookseller, brought me a "pacquet left with him; it contained an ode, or little "poem,

nious and virtuous youth. I reluctantly
proceed to develope the only circumftance
which

" poem, of two or three ftanzas in alternate rhyme, on the
" death of Richard the Firft, and I was told, in very few
" lines, that it had been found at Briftol, with many other
" old poems, and that the poffeffor could furnifh me with
" accounts of a feries of great painters, who had flourifhed
" at Briftol.

" Here I muft paufe, to mention my own reflections.
" At firft I concluded that fomebody having met with my
" Anecdotes of Painting, had a mind to laugh at me ; I
" thought not very ingenuoufly, as I was not likely to
" fwallow a fucceffion of great painters at Briftol. The
" ode, or fonnet *, as I think it was called, was too pretty
" to be part of the plan ; and, as is eafy with all the other
" fuppofed poems of Rowley, it was not difficult to make it
" modern by changing the old words for new, though yet
" more difficult than with moft of them. You fee I tell you
" fairly the cafe.

" I wrote, according to the inclofed direction, for farther
" particulars. Chatterton, in anfwer, informed me that
" he was the fon of a poor widow, who fupported him with
" great difficulty ; that he was clerk or apprentice to an at-
" torney, but had a tafte and turn for more elegant ftudies ;
" and hinted a wifh that I would affift him with my intereft
" in emerging out of fo dull a profeffion, by procuring
" him fome place, in which he could purfue his natural
" bent. He affirmed that great treafures of ancient poetry
                                                    " had

* " Richard of Lyon's Heart to fight is gone."

which has involved his name and character in difgrace, and which certainly de-
                                    prived

" had been difcovered in his native city, and were in the
" hands of a *perfon*, who had lent him thofe he had tranf-
" mitted to me ; for he now fent me others, amongft which
" was an abfolute modern paftoral in dialogue, thinly
" fprinkled with old words *. Pray obferve, Sir, that he
" affirmed having received the poems from another perfon ;
" whereas it is afcertained that the gentleman at Briftol,
" who poffeffes the fund of Rowley's poems, received them
" from Chatterton.
" I wrote to a relation of mine at Bath, to enquire into
" the fituation and character of Chatterton, according to
" his own account of himfelf ; nothing was returned about
" his character, but his ftory was verified.
" In the mean time I communicated the poems to Mr.
" Gray and Mr. Mafon, who at once pronounced them
" forgeries, and declared there was no fymptom in them of
" their being the productions of, near fo diftant an age ; the
" language and metres being totally unlike any thing an-
" cient.
" Well, Sir, being fatisfied with my intelligence about
" Chatterton, I wrote him a letter with as much kindnefs
" and tendernefs as if I had been his guardian ; for though
" I had no doubt of his impofitions, fuch a fpirit of poetry
" breathed in his coinage, as interefted me for him ; nor
" was it a grave crime in a young bard to have forged falfe
" notes of hand, that were to pafs current only in the parifh
                                    " of

* Elinoure and Juga.

prived the world prematurely of his excellent abilities? When or how he was unfortunate

"of Parnaſſus." I undecived him about my being a perſon
"of any intereſt; and urged, that in duty and gratitude to
"his mother, who had ſtraitened herſelf to breed him up to
"a profeſſion, he ought to labour in it, that in her old age
"he might abſolve his filial debt; and I told him, that
"when he ſhould have made a fortune, he might unbend
"himſelf with the ſtudies conſonant to his inclinations. I
"told him alſo, that I had communicated his tranſcripts to
"better judges, and that they were by no means ſatisfied
"with the authenticity of his ſuppoſed MSS. He wrote
"me rather a peeviſh anſwer, ſaid he could not conteſt with
"a perſon of my learning, (a compliment by no means due
"to me, and which I certainly had not aſſumed, having
"mentioned my having conſulted abler judges,) main-
"tained the genuineneſs of the poems, and demanded to
"have them returned, *as they were the property of another*
"*gentleman.* Remember this.
"When I received this letter, I was going to Paris in a
"day or two, and either forgot his requeſt of the poems,
"or perhaps not having time to have them copied,
"deferred complying till my return, which was to be in
"ſix weeks. I proteſt I do not remember which was the
"caſe; and yet, though in a cauſe of ſo little importance,
"I will not utter a ſyllable of which I am not poſitively
"certain, nor will not charge my memory with a tittle be-
"yond what it retains. Soon after my return from France,
"I received another letter from Chatterton, the ſtyle of
"which was ſingularly impertinent. He demanded his
"poems

fortunate enough to receive a tincture of infidelity, we are not informed. Early in

the

"poems roughly; and added, that I should not have dared
"to use him so ill, if he had not acquainted me with the
"narrowness of his circumstances My heart did not accuse
"me of insolence to him. I wrote an answer to him, ex-
"postulating with him on his injustice, and renewing good
"advice; but upon second thoughts, reflecting that so
"wrong-headed a young man, of whom I knew nothing,
"and whom I had never seen, might be absurd enough to
"print my letter, I flung it into the fire; and wrapping up
"both his poems and letters, without taking a copy of
"either, for which I am now sorry, I returned all to him,
"and thought no more about him or them, till about a year
"and a half after, when dining at the Royal Academy,
"Dr. Goldsmith drew the attention of the company with
"an account of a marvellous treasure of ancient poems
"lately discovered at Bristol, and expressed enthusiastic be-
"lief in them, for which he was laughed at by Dr. John-
"son, who was present. I soon found this was the trou-
"vaille of my friend Chatterton; and I told Dr. Goldsmith
"that this novelty was none to me, who might, if I had
"pleased, have had the honour of ushering the great dif-
"covery to the learned world. You may imagine, Sir,
"we did not at all agree in the measure of our faith; but
"though his credulity diverted me, my mirth was soon
"dashed; for on asking about Chatterton, he told me he
"had been in London, and had destroyed himself. I
"heartily wished then that I had been the dupe of all the
"poor young man had written to me; for who would not

"have

the year 1769, it appears from a poem on
Happiness, addressed to Mr. Catcott, that
he

" have his understanding imposed upon to save a fellow
" being from the utmost wretchedness, despair, and suicide !
" and a poor young man, not eighteen, and of such miracu-
" lous talents ; for, dear Sir, if I wanted credulity on
" one hand, it is ample on the other. Yet heap all the
" improbabilities you please on the head of Chatterton, the
" impossibility on Rowley's side will remain. An amazing
" genius for poetry, which one of them possessed, might
" flash out in the darkest age ; but could Rowley anticipate
" the phraseology of the eighteenth century ? His poetic
" fire might burst through the obstacles of the times ; like
" Homer, or other original bards, he might have formed
" a poetical style ; but would it have been precisely that
" of an age subsequent to him by some hundred years ?
" Nobody can admire the poetry of the poems in question
" more than I do, but except being better than most mo-
" dern verses, in what do they differ in the construction ?
" The words are old, the construction evidently of yester-
" day ; and, by substituting modern words, aye, single
" words, to the old, or to those invented by Chatterton ;
" in what do they differ ? Try that method with any com-
" position, even in prose, of the reign of Henry VI. and
" see if the consequence will be the same. But I am get-
" ting into the controversy, instead of concluding my nar-
" rative, which indeed is ended."

Whatever imputation might have lain on Mr. Walpole
with regard to the treatment of Chatterton, before these
particulars were known, and this narrative appeared, surely
there

he had drank deeply of the poifoned
fpring: And in the conclufion of a letter
to

there can be no impartial reader of it who will not acquit
him of any ill treatment of a perfon who appeared to him in
fo queftionable a fhape; and allow that in Mr. Walpole's
fituation, he could fcarcely have acted otherwife than he did.
For what was the cafe? A youth of fixteen years of age,
clerk to an attorney at Briftol, totally unknown to Mr.
Walpole, fends him a letter, acquainting him that the
writer, though bred to the law, had a tafte for politer ftudies,
particularly poetry, and wifhed to be drawn out of his
prefent fituation, and placed in one more at his eafe,
where he might purfue the ftudies more congenial to his tafte
and genius; but of this tafte and genius he produces no other
proof than tranfcripts of fome old poems, faid to have been
found at Briftol, and to be *the property of another perfon.*
Thefe poems being exhibited by Mr. Walpole to Mr. Gray
and Mr. Mafon, thefe excellent and impartial judges agreed
in opinion that they muft be modern productions, difguifed
in antiquated phrafes; and, with regard to a long lift of
Briftol artifts, carvellers and painters, announced alfo as
part of this treafure, Mr. Walpole was as confident that
none fuch ever had any exiftence, and therefore he could
not help concluding that the whole was a fiction, contrived
by fome one or more literary wags, who wifhed to impofe
on his credulity, and to laugh at him if they fucceeded, and
that Chatterton was only the inftrument employed to introduce and recommend thefe old writings. His youth and
fituation could not lead Mr. Walpole to fuppofe he was
himfelf the author and contriver, more efpecially as he had
afferted

to the same gentleman, after he left Bristol, he expresses himself: " Heaven send
you

afserted them to be the property of a person at Bristol then
alive. He had indeed represented himself as a lover of
the muses, but had given no specimens of his *own* compositions: The kindest thing therefore Mr. Walpole could do
for a young man in this situation, was, after a gentle hint
of his suspicions of the authenticity of the poems, to recommend to his correspondent to pursue the line of business
in which he was placed, as most likely to secure a decent
maintenance for himself, and enable him to assist his mother. However disappointed Chatterton might have been
at the time, and angry with Mr. Walpole for this rebuff,
it should seem as if he had not harboured any long or strong
resentment against that gentleman; for in a copy of verses
addressed to Miss M. R. and sent by him to the Town and
Country Magazine, and printed in the Number for January
1770, is the following stanza:

<blockquote>

" Yet when that bloom and dancing fire,
" In silver'd reverence shall expire,
" Aged, wrinkled, and defac'd,
" To keep one lover's flame alive
" Requires the genius of a *Clive*,
" With WALPOLE's mental taste.

</blockquote>

See Chatterton's Miscellanies, p. 88.

It should seem also, that Chatterton had in part adopted
Mr. Walpole's advice, by continuing with his master a full
twelvemonth after his application to that gentlemen. Then
he

you the comforts of Chriftianity; I requeft them not, for I am no Chriftian."
                                    Infidelity,

he got difmiffed from his mafter and went to London, in full confidence that his literary talents would find ample employment
and encouragement from the London bookfellers; but being
difappointed in his expectation, the fatal conclufion which has
juft been mentioned took place. Had this been the cafe immediately on his receipt of Mr. Walpole's laft letter, fome fhadow
of foundation might have appeared for the harfh cenfures
paffed on Mr. Walpole's treatment of this ill-fated youth;
though even then, no real one, all circumftances confidered.

From the fpirited reply of Mr. Walpole to one of thefe
cenfurers, (the Editor of Chatterton's Mifcellanies,) and
printed in the fame pamphlet as the letter to W. B. the
following extract is given, as equally applicable to all objectors.

" Was it the part of a juft man to couple Chatterton's
" firft unfuccefsful application with his fatal exit, and load
" me with both? Does your enthufiaftic admiration of
" his abilities; or your regrets for the honour of England's
" poetry, warrant fuch a concatenation of ideas? Was
" poor Chatterton fo modeft, or fo defponding, as to aban-
" don his enterprizes on their being damped by me? Did
" he not continue to purfue them? Is this country fo defti-
" tute of patrons of genius, or do I move in fo eminent and
" diftinguifhed a fphere, that a repulfe from me is a dagger
" to talents? Did not Chatterton come to London after
" that mifcarriage? Did he relinquifh his counterfeiting
" propenfity on its being loft on me? Was he an inoffen-

F   " five

Infidelity, or scepticism at least, may be termed the disease of young, lively, and half-informed minds. There is something like

" five ingenuous youth, smit with the love of the muses,
" and soaring above a sordid and servile profession, whose
" early blossoms being blighted by my insolence, withered
" in mortified obscurity, and on seeing his hopes of fame
" blasted, sunk beneath the frowns of ignorant and insolent
" wealth? or did he, after launching into all the excesses
" you describe, and vainly hoping to gratify his ambition
" by adulation to, or satires on all ranks and parties of
" men, fall a victim to his own ungovernable spirit, and to
" the deplorable straits to which he had reduced himself?
" The interval was short, I own; but as every moment of
" so extraordinary a life was crouded with efforts of his en-
" terprising genius, allow me to say with truth, that there
" was a large chasm between his application to me and his
" miserable conclusion. You know there was; and though
" my falling into his snare might have varied the æra of
" his exploits, it is more likely that that success would
" rather have encouraged than checked his enterprises.
" When he pursued his turn for fabricating ancient writings,
" in spite of the mortification he received from me, it is
" not probable that he would have been corrected by suc-
" cess; such is not the nature of success, when it is the
" reward of artifice. I should be more justly reproachable
" for having contributed to cherish an impostor, than I am
" for having accelerated his fate. I cannot repeat the
" words without emotions of indignation on my own ac-
" count, and of compassion on his." O.

like difcovery in the rejection of truths to
which they have been from infancy in
trammels. A little learning, too, mifleads
the underftanding, in an opinion of its
own powers. When we have acquired
the outlines of fcience, we are apt to fuppofe that every thing is within our com-
prehenfion. Much ftudy and much information are required to difcover the difficulties in which the fyftems of infidels
are involved. There are profound, as well
as popular arguments, in favour of revealed
religion; but when the flippancy of Vol-
taire or Hume has taught young perfons
to fuppofe that they have defeated the former, their underftandings feldom recover
fufficient vigour to purfue the latter with
the ability and perfeverance of a Newton
or a Bryant.

The evil effect of thefe principles upon
the morals of youth, is often found to fur-
vive the fpeculative impreffions which they

have

have made on the intellect. Wretched
is that person, who, in the ardour and
impetuosity of youth, finds himself re-
leased from all the salutary restraints
of duty and religion; wretched is he,
who, deprived of all the comforting
hopes of another state, is reduced to seek
for happiness in the vicious gratifications
of this life; who, under such delusions,
acquires habits of profligacy or discontent!
The progress, however, from speculative
to practical irreligion, is not so rapid as is
commonly supposed. The greatest advantage of a strict and orderly education is the
resistance which virtuous habits, early acquired, oppose to the allurements of vice.
Those who have sullied the youth of Chatterton with the imputation of extraordinary vices or irregularities, and have asserted, that " his profligacy was, at least, as
conspicuous as his abilities *," have, I
conceive, rather grounded these assertions

on

* Preface to Chatterton's Miscellanies, p. 18.

on the apparently profane and immoral
tendency of some of his productions, than
on personal knowledge or a correct review of his conduct. During his residence
at Bristol, we have the most respectable
evidence in favour of the regularity of his
conduct, namely, that of his master, Mr.
Lambert. Of few young men in his situation it can be said, that during a course
of nearly three years, he seldom encroach-
ed upon the strict limits which were
assigned him, with respect to his hours of
liberty; that his master could never accuse
him of improper behaviour, and that he
had the utmost reason to be satisfied he
never spent his hours of leisure in any but
respectable company.

Mrs. Newton, with that unaffected sim-
plicity which so eminently characterises her
letter, most powerfully controverts the
obloquy which had been thrown upon
her brother's memory. She says, that
while he was at Mr. Lambert's, he visited

F 3 his

his mother regularly most evenings before nine o'clock, and they were seldom two evenings together without seeing him. He was for a considerable time remarkably indifferent to females. He declared to his sister, that he had always seen the whole sex with perfect indifference, except those whom nature had rendered dear. He remarked, at the same time, the tendency of severe study to sour the temper, and indicated his inclination to form an acquaintance with a young female in the neighbourhood, apprehending that it might soften that austerity of temper which had resulted from solitary study. The juvenile Petrarch wanted a Laura, to polish his manners and exercise his fancy. He addressed a poem to Miss Rumsey; and they commenced, Mrs. Newton adds, a corresponding acquaintance. "He would also frequently," she says, "walk the College Green with the young girls that statedly paraded there to shew their finery;"

finery * ;" but she is perfuaded that the reports which charge him with libertinifm are ill-founded †. She could not perhaps have added a better proof of it, than his inclination to affociate with modeft women. The teftimony of Mr. Thiftlethwaite is not lefs explicit or lefs honourable to Chatterton. " The opportunities," fays he, " which a long acquaintance with him

F 4   afforded

---

* In a letter from London to his fifter, he particularizes ten Briftol females of his acquaintance, and adds, " I promifed to write to fome hundreds, I believe ; but what with writing for publications, and going to places of public diverfion, which is as abfolutely neceffary to me as my food, I find but little time to write to you." O.

† Mrs. Newton's letter. I cannot help remarking a pleafant miftake of the Dean of Exeter: The orthography of Mrs. N. in the letter printed in Love and Madnefs, is not the moft correct. Her words are, " I really believe he was no debauchee (though fome have reported it) ; the dear unhappy boy had faults enough, I faw with concern ; he was proud and exceedingly imperious, but that of *venality* he could not be juftly accufed with." It is eafy to fee that Mrs. N. by *venality* means libertinifm ; but the Dean taking the word in the ufual fenfe, makes ufe of it to difprove, what is feldom fufpected of a poet, and leaft of all of Chatterton, that he was avaricious.

afforded me, juftify me in faying, that
whilft he lived at Briftol, he was not the
debauched character he has been reprefented. Temperate in his living, moderate in
his pleafures, and regular in his exercifes,
he was undeferving of the afperfion. I
admit that amongft his papers may be
found many paffages, not only immoral,
but bordering upon a libertinifm grofs and
unpardonable. It is not my intention to
attempt a vindication of thofe paffages,
which, for the regard I bear his memory,
I wifh he had never written, but which I
neverthelefs believe to have originated rather from a warmth of imagination, aided
by a vain affectation of fingularity, than
from any natural depravity, or from a heart
vitiated by evil example *."

But

---

* Milles's Rowley, p. 461. Whether the following paffage from Chatterton's Kew Gardens (a poem not publifhed
in any of the collections of his works) be received as a confirmation of his friend's teftimony in his favour, or the contrary,

But though it may not always be the effect of infidel principles, to plunge the person who becomes unfortunately infected with them into an immediate course of flagrant and shameless depravity, they seldom

trary, it is, however, worth preserving. An officious friend is introduced accosting him in the following lines:

" Is there a street within this spacious place,
" That boasts the happiness of one fair face,
" Whose conversation does not turn on you?
" Blaming your wild amours, and morals too.
" Oaths, sacred and tremendous oaths you swear,
" Oaths which might shock a L——'s soul to hear;
" Whilst the too tender and believing maid,
" Remember pretty —— is betray'd.
" Then your religion!—oh, beware! beware!
" Although a Deist is no monster here,
" Think not the merit of a jingling song
" Can countenance the author's acting wrong.
" Reform your manners, and with solemn air,
" Hear Catcott bray, and Robins squeak in prayer.
" Damn'd narrow notions, notions which disgrace
" The boasted freedom of the human race;
" Bristol may keep her prudent maxims still,
" I scorn her prudence, and I ever will.
" Since all my vices magnified are here,
" She cannot paint me worse than I appear.
" When raving in the lunacy of ink,
" I catch the pen, and publish what I think." O.

dom fail to unhinge the mind, and render
it the sport of some passion, unfriendly to
our happiness and prosperity. One of their
first effects in Chatterton was to render the
idea of suicide familiar, and to dispose
him to think lightly of the most sacred
deposit with which man is entrusted by
his Creator. It has been supposed that
his violent death in London, was the sudden or almost instant effect of extreme
poverty and disappointment. It appears,
however, that long before he left Bristol,
he had repeatedly intimated to the servants
of Mr. Lambert, his intention of putting
an end to his existence. Mr. Lambert's
mother was particularly terrified, but she
was unable to persuade her son of the
reality of his threats, till he found by accident upon his desk a paper, entitled,
the " Last Will and Testament of Thomas
Chatterton *," in which he seriously indicated

* See the Will in the Appendix to Chatterton's Misc.

cated his defign of committing suicide on
the following day, namely, Eafter Sunday, April 15th, 1770. The paper was,
probably rather the refult of temporary
uneafinefs *, than of that fixed averfion to
his fituation which he conftantly manifefted; but with principles and paffions fuch
as Chatterton difplayed, Mr. Lambert
confidered it as no longer prudent, after
fo decifive a proof, to continue him in the
houfe; he accordingly difmiffed him immediately from his fervice, in which he
had continued two years, nine months,
and thirteen days.

If there was any fincerity in the intentions of committing fuicide, which he expreffed in the paper above alluded to, he was
diverted from it for the prefent by the gold-
en profpects with which he flattered himfelf from a new plan of life, on which he
entered

---

* I have been informed from good authority, that it was
occafioned by the refufal of a gentleman, whom he had occafionally complimented in his poems, to accommodate him
with a fupply of money.

entered with his ufual enthufiafm. A few months before he left Briftol, he had written letters to feveral bookfellers in London*, "who," Mr. Thiftlethwaite fays, "finding him of advantage to them in their publications, were by no means fparing of their praifes and compliments; adding the moft liberal promifes of affiftance and employment, fhould he choofe to make London the place of his refidence †." To the interrogatories of this gentleman concerning the plan of life which he intended to purfue on his arrival at London, his anfwer was remarkable, and correfponds with what has been juft related. "My firft attempt," faid he, "fhall be in the literary way: The promifes I have received are fufficient to difpel doubt; but fhould I, contrary to my expectation, find myfelf deceived, I will in that cafe turn Methodift preacher: Credulity is as potent a deity as ever, and a new

* Mrs. Newton's Letter.
† Milles's Rowley, p. 460.

new fect may eafily be devifed. But if that too fhould fail me, my laft and final refource is a piftol."

Before he quitted Briftol, he had entered deeply into politics, and had embraced what was termed the patriotic party. In March 1770, he wrote a fatirical poem, called "Kew Gardens," confifting of above 1300 lines. This he tranfmitted, in different packets, to Mr. George William Edmunds, No. 73, Shoe-lane, Printer of a patriotic newfpaper. At the bottom of the firft packet, which contained about 300 lines, written in Chatterton's own hand, is this poftfcript. "Mr. Edmunds will fend the author, Thomas Chatterton, twenty of the Journals, in which the above poem (which I fhall continue) fhall appear, by the machine, if he thinks proper to put it in; the money fhall be paid to his orders." The poem is a fatire on the Princefs Dowager of Wales,

Lord

Lord Bute, and their Friends in London
and Briftol, but particularly on thofe in
Briftol, who had diftinguifhed themfelves
in favour of the Miniftry. His fignature
on this occafion was DECIMUS; but whether the poem was ever printed or not, I
have not been able to afcertain. I have
been alfo informed of another political
fatire of near 600 lines, the manufcript of
which, in Chatterton's hand-writing, is
in the poffeffion of a friend of Mr. Catcott.
It is called "The Whore of Babylon."
The fatire of this poem is alfo directed
againft the Miniftry, and, like the former,
it includes feveral of the Briftol people,
not excepting Mr. George Catcott, and
his brother the clergyman. But his party
efforts were not confined altogether to
poetry; he wrote an invective in profe
againft Bifhop Newton, alfo figned Decimus, which, I believe, appeared in fome
of the periodical publications of the times.

The

The manuscript of this letter is in Mr.
Catcott's possession; but the style appears
much inferior to that of his prose publications posterior to his arrival in London.
To write well in prose is perhaps more
the effect of art, of study, and of habit, than
of natural genius. The rules of metrical
composition are fewer, more simple, and
require a less constant exercise of the judgment. In the infancy of societies, as well
as of individuals, therefore, the art of
poetry is antecedent to those of rhetoric
and criticism, and arrives at perfection
long before the language of prose attains
that degree of strength, concifeness, and
harmony, which is requisite to satisfy a
delicate ear. Chatterton wrote also an
indecent satirical poem, called " The Exhibition," occasioned by the improper
behaviour of a person in Bristol. The
satire of this poem is chiefly local, and the
characters of most of the surgeons in Bristol

are delineated in it. Some defcriptive
paffages in this poem have great merit.
Thus, fpeaking of a favourite organift,
probably Mr. Allen, he fays:

" He keeps the paffions with the found in play,
" And the foul trembles with the trembling key *."

There are a number of other unpublifh-
ed works of his difperfed in the hands of
different perfons. The activity of his
mind is indeed almoft unparalleled. But
our furprife muft decreafe, when we confider that he flept but little; and that his
whole attention was directed to literary
purfuits; for he declares himfelf fo ignorant of his profeffion, that he was unable
to draw out a clearance from his appren-
ticefhip, which Mr. Lambert demanded †.
He was alfo unfettered by the ftudy of the
dead languages, which ufually abforb much

of

* Love and Madnefs, p. 167.
† See the third letter of Chatterton, publifhed in Love
and Madnefs, p. 198.

of the time and attention of young perfons; and though they may be useful to
the attainment of correctnefs, perhaps
they do not much contribute to fluency in
writing. Mr. Catcott declared, that when
he firft knew Chatterton, he was ignorant
even of Grammar *.

There are three great æras in the life of
Chatterton, his admiffion into Colfton's
fchool, his being put apprentice to Mr.
Lambert, and his expedition to London.
In the latter end of April, 1770, he bade
his native city (from which he had never
previoufly been abfent further than he
could walk in half a Sunday) *a final
adieu* †. In a letter to his mother, dated
April 26th, he defcribes in a lively ftyle
the little adventures of his journey, and
his reception from his patrons, the bookfellers and printers with whom he had

G cor-

---

* From the information of Mr. Seward.
† Love and Madnefs, p. 191.

corresponded; these were Mr. Edmunds, whom I lately had occasion to mention as a noted patriotic printer at that period; Mr. Fell, publisher of the Freeholder's Magazine; Mr. Hamilton, proprietor of the Town and Country; and Mr. Dodsley, of Pall-Mall. From all of them he professes to have received great encouragement, adding, that all approved of his design, and that he should probably be soon settled. In the same letter, he desires his mother to call upon Mr. Lambert. "Shew him this," says he, with uncommon dignity and spirit, "or tell him, if I deserve a recommendation, he would oblige me to give me one—if I do not, it would be beneath him to take notice of me*."

His first habitation after his arrival in London was at Mr. Walmsley's, a plaisterer in Shoreditch, to whom he was introduced by a relation of his, a Mrs. Ballance, who

* Love and Madness, p. 192.

who refided in the fame houfe. Of his firft eftablifhment, his report is favourable. " I am fettled," fays he, in a letter to his mother, dated May 6th, " and in fuch a fettlement as I could defire. I get four guineas a month by one magazine; fhall engage to write a hiftory of England, and other pieces, which will more than double that fum. Occafional effays for the daily papers would more than fupport me. What a glorious profpect * !" In confequence of his engagements with the different magazines, we find him, about the fame time, foliciting communications from his poetical and literary friends at Briftol, and defiring them to read the Freeholder's Magazine. In a letter dated the 14th of the fame month, he writes in the fame high flow of fpirits: He fpeaks of the great encouragement which genius meets with in London; adding, with exultation,

" If

* Love and Madnefs. p. 107.

" If Rowley had been a Londoner inftead
of a Briftowyan; I might have lived by
copying his works. *" He exhorts his fifter
to "improve in copying mufic, drawing,
and every thing which requires genius;"
obferving that although, " in Briftol's
mercantile ftyle, thofe things may be ufelefs, if not a detriment to her; *here*
they are very profitable †." His engagements at that period indeed appear to
have been numerous; for befides his employment in the magazines, he fpeaks of
a connection which he had formed with
a doctor in mufic, to write fongs for Ranelagh, Vauxhall, &c.; and in a letter
of the 30th to his fifter, he mentions
another with a Scottifh bookfeller, to com-
pile a voluminous hiftory of London, to
appear in numbers, for which he was to
have

---

* Yet it does not appear that any of Rowley's pieces were
exhibited after C. left Briftol.   O.

† Love and Madnefs, p. 201.

have his board at the bookſeller's houſe, and a handſome premium *.

Party writing, however, ſeems to have been one of his favourite employments. It was agreeable to the ſatirical turn of his diſpoſition, and it gratified his vanity, by the proſpect of elevating him into immediate notice. When his relation, Mrs. Ballance, recommended it to him to endeavour to get into ſome office, he ſtormed like a madman, and alarmed the good old lady in no inconſiderable degree, by telling her, " he hoped, with the bleſſing of God, very ſoon to be ſent priſoner to the Tower, which would make his fortune." In his ſecond letter to his mother from London, he ſays, " Mr. Wilkes knew me by my writings, ſince I firſt

G 3   cor-

* Love and Madneſs, p. 202. The Editor of Chatterton's Miſcellanies confounds this with Northook's Hiſtory of London; but that gentleman, in a letter printed in the St. James's Chronicle, denies having ever had the leaſt knowledge of C. Indeed the ſcheme above alluded to appears not to have been proceeded in.

corresponded with the bookſellers here.
I ſhall viſit him next week, and by his intereſt will inſure Mrs. Ballance the Trinity Houſe. He affirmed that what Mr.
Fell had of mine could not be the writings
of a youth, and expreſſed a deſire to know
the author. By means of another bookſeller, I ſhall be introduced to Townſhend,
and Sawbridge. I am quite familiar at the
Chapter Coffee-houſe, and know all the
geniuſſes there. A character is now unneceſſary; an author carries his character
in his pen *." He informs his ſiſter that,
if money flowed as faſt upon him as honours, he would give her a portion of five
thouſand pounds. This extraordinary elevation of ſpirits aroſe from an introduction
to the celebrated patriotic Lord Mayor,
W. Beckford. Chatterton had, it ſeems,
addreſſed an eſſay to him, which was ſo
well received, that it encouraged him to
wait

* Love and Madneſs, p. 194.

upon his Lordſhip, in order to obtain his approbation to addreſs a ſecond letter to him,
on the ſubject of the city remonſtrance,
and its reception. "His Lordſhip (adds
he) received me as politely as a citizen
could, and warmly invited me to call on
him again. The reſt is a ſecret." His
inclination doubtleſs led him to eſpouſe
the party of oppoſition ; but he complains,
that " no money is to be got on that ſide
the queſtion ; intereſt is on the other ſide.
But he is a poor author who cannot write,
on both ſides. I believe I may be introduced (and if I am not, I'll introduce myſelf) to a ruling power in the Court
party.* When Beckford died, he is ſaid
to have been almoſt frantic †, and to have
exclaimed, that he was ruined. The elegy,
however, in which he has celebrated him ‡,

G 4 contains

* Love and Madneſs, p. 203.
† Ibid. p. 214.
‡ Chat. Miſcel. p. 76.

contains more of frigid praise, than of ardent feeling; nor is there in it a single
line which appears to flow from the heart.
Indeed, that he was serious in his intention of writing on both sides, is evident
from a lift of pieces written by Chatterton,
but never published, which Mr. Walpole
has preserved. No. V. of these pieces is
a letter to Lord North, dated May 26th,
1770, signed *Moderator*, and beginning,
" My Lord, It gives me a painful plea-
sure, &c." It contains, as Mr. Walpole
informs us, an encomium on Administra-
tion for rejecting the City Remonstrance.
On the other hand, No. VI. is a letter to
the Lord Mayor, Beckford, (probably that
which he desired his permission to address
to him). It is also dated May 26, signed
Probus, and contains a virulent invective
against Government for rejecting the Remonstrance, beginning, " When the endeavours of a spirited people to free them-
selves

felves from infupportable flavery, &c." On
the back of this effay, which is directed
to Mr. Cary, a particular friend of Chatterton in Briftol, is this indorfement :
" Accepted by Bingley—fet for, and
thrown out of the North Briton, 21ft
June, on account of the Lord Mayor's
death.

Loft by his death on this Effay,	£. 1	11	6
Gained in Elegies,	£. 2	2	0
—— In Effays,	3	3	0
	5	5	0
Am glad he is dead by —	£. 3	13	6*"

" Effays," again fays he to his fifter,
" on the patriotic fide, fetch no more than
what the copy is fold for. As the patriots
themfelves are fearching for a place, they
have no gratuities to fpare. On the other
hand, unpopular effays will not even be
accepted, and you muft pay to have them
printed ;

* Two letters printed at Strawberry-hill.

printed; but then you feldom lofe by it. Courtiers are fo fenfible of their deficiency in merit, that they generally reward all who know how to daub them with an appearance of it *." Either Chatterton, on this occafion, fpoke from hear-fay, or there is reafon to believe that the minif-terial arrangements are greatly altered in this refpect, and that moft of the late ad-miniftrations have found a more effectual, if a more expenfive fupport, from a venal majority in the Houfe, than from a venal phalanx of mendicant authors in the daily papers.

On this fandy foundation of party writ-ing Chatterton erected a vifionary fabric of future greatnefs; and, in the waking dreams of a poetical imagination, he was already a man of confiderable public importance. It was a common affertion with him, " that he would fettle the nation before he had

had done *." In a letter to his sister of the 20th July, he tells her, " My company is courted every where; and, could I humble myself to go into a compter, could have had twenty places before now; but I must be among the great; state matters suit me better than commercial †." In a former letter he intimates, that he " might have had a recommendation to Sir George Cole-brooke, an East-India Director, as quali-fied for an office no ways despicable, but," he adds, " I shall not take a step to the sea, whilst I can continue on land ‡." His taste for dissipation seems to have kept pace with the increase of his vanity. To frequent places of public amusement, he accounts as necessary to him as food. " I employ my money," says he, " now in fitting myself fashionably, and getting

into

---

* Love and Madness, p. 214.
† Ibid. p. 210.
‡ Ibid. p. 203.
‖ Ibid. p. 200.

into good company; this laft article always
brings me in intereft *."

While engaged in the examination of
thefe curious letters, it is impoffible not
to be attracted by a remarkable paffage.
Chatterton informs his mother in the letter of May 14th, " A gentleman, who
knows me at the Chapter, as an author,
would have introduced me as a companion
to the young Duke of Northumberland,
in his intended general tour; but, alas!
I fpeak no tongue but my own †." It is
not very credible, that any of the conftant
frequenters of the Chapter Coffee-houfe
fhould be poffeffed of influence fufficient
to recommend a perfon to the Duke of
Northumberland, to fo important an office
as that of the care of his fon; much lefs
credible is it, that fuch a perfon would
recommend a young literary adventurer,
whofe

---

whofe character was only known by an
accidental meeting at a coffee-houfe; and
leaft credible of all it is, that fuch a perfon
was likely to be accepted on fo flender a
ground of recommendation. It is no un-
frequent fport with little minds to play
with the fanguine tempers and expectations
of young and unexperienced minds : Poor
Chatterton had tolerable experience of
thefe prodigal promifers, from the patriotic
Beckford to his pretended patron at the
Chapter Coffee-houfe.

The fplendid vifions of promotion and
confequence however foon vanifhed, and
our adventurer found no patrons but the
bookfellers; and even here he feems not
to have efcaped the poignant fting of dif-
appointment. Soon after his arrival in
London, he writes to his mother, " The
poverty of authors is a common obfervation, but not always a true one. No
author can be poor who underftands the
arts

arts of bookſellers; without this neceſſary
knowledge the greateſt genius may ſtarve,
and with it the greateſt dunce may live in
ſplendour. This knowledge I have pretty
well dipped into *." This knowledge,
however, inſtead of conducting to opulence
and independence, proved a deluſive guide;
and though he boaſts of having pieces in
the month of June 1770 in the Goſpel
Magazine, the Town and Country, the
Court and City, the London, the Political
Regiſter, &c. and that almoſt the whole
Town and Country for the following month
was his †; yet it appears, ſo ſcanty is the
remuneration for thoſe periodical labours,
that even theſe uncommon exertions of
induſtry and genius were inſufficient to
ward off the approach of poverty; and he
ſeems to have ſunk almoſt at once from
the higheſt elevation of hope and illuſion,

to

* Love and Madneſs, p. 195.
† Ibid. p. 210.

to the depths of defpair. Early in July
he removed his lodgings from Shoreditch
to Mrs. Angel's, a fack-maker in Brook-
ftreet, Holborn. Mr. Walmfley's family
affirmed that he affigned no reafon for
quitting their houfe. The author of Love
and Madnefs attributes the change to the
neceffity he was under, from the nature of
his employments, of frequenting public
places *. Is it not probable that he
might remove, left his friends in Shoreditch, who had heard his frequent boafts,
and obferved his dream of greatnefs, fhould
be the fpectators of his approaching indigence ? Pride was the ruling paffion of
Chatterton, and a too acute fenfe of fhame,
is ever found to accompany literary pride.
But however he might be defirous of pre-
ferving appearances to the world, he was
fufficiently lowered in his own expectations ; and great indeed muft have been
his

* Love and Madnefs, p. 189.

his humiliation, when we find his tower-
ing ambition reduced to the miserable hope
of securing the very ineligible appointment
of a surgeon's mate to Africa. To his
friend Mr. Barrett he applied in his dif-
tress for a recommendation to this un-
promising station. Even in this dreary
prospect he was not, however, without
the consolations of his muse; his fancy
delighted itself with the expectation of
contemplating the wonders of a country,
where " Nature flourishes in her most
perfect vigour; where the *purple* aloe,
and the scarlet jeffamine, diffuse their rich
perfumes; where the reeking tygers bask
in the sedges, or wanton with their shadows
in the stream."*

His resolution was announced in a poem
to Miss Bush,† in the style of Cowley, that
is, with too much affectation of wit for real
feeling.

* See the African Eclogues, Chat. Misc. p. 56—61.
† Chat. Misc. p. 85.

feeling. Probably, indeed, when he composed the African Eclogues, which was
just before, he might not be without a
distant contemplation of a similar design;
and perhaps we are to attribute a part of
the exulting expressions, which occur in
the letters to his mother and sister, to the
kind and laudable intention of making
them happy with respect to his profpects in life; since we find him, almost
at the very crisis of his distress, sending a
number of little unnecessary presents to
them and his grandmother, while perhaps
he was himself almost in want of the ne-
cessaries of life.

On the score of incapacity probably,
Mr. Barrett refused him the necessary recommendation, and his last hope was blasted*. Of Mrs. Angel, with whom he

H last

* This circumstance reflects no disgrace, but rather honour upon Mr. B. as he could not possibly foresee the melancholy consequence, and he could not in conscience be the
                                         instrument

laft refided, no enquiries have afforded
any fatisfactory intelligence; but there
can be little doubt that his death was pre-
ceded by extreme indigence. Mr. Crofs,
an apothecary in Brook-ftreet, informed
Mr. Warton, that while Chatterton lived
in the neighbourhood, he frequently called
at the fhop, and was repeatedly preffed by
Mr. Crofs to dine or fup with him in vain.
One evening, however, human frailty fo
far prevailed over his dignity, as to tempt
him to partake of the regale of a bar-
rel of oyfters, when he was obferved to
eat moft voracioufly †. Mrs. Wolfe, a
barber's wife, within a few doors of the
houfe where Mrs. Angel lived, has alfo
afforded ample teftimony, both to his poverty and his pride. She fays, " that
Mrs. Angel told her, after his death, that
on the 24th of Auguft, as fhe knew he
had

---

inftrument of committing the lives of a confiderable number
of perfons to one totally inadequate to the charge.

† Warton's Inquiry, p. 107.

had not eaten any thing for two or three days, fhe begged he would take fome din-ner with her; but he was offended at her expreffions, which feemed to hint he was in want, and affured her he was not hungry *." In thefe defperate circum-ftances, his mind reverted to what (we learn from Mr. Thiftlethwaite, and other quarters) he had accuftomed himfelf to regard as a laft refource.—" Over his death, for the fake of the world," fays the author of Love and Madnefs, " I would willingly draw a veil. But this muft not be. They who are in a condition to patronife merit, and they who feel a con-fcioufnefs of merit which is not patronifed, may form their own refolutions from the cataftrophe of his tale ;—thofe, to lofe no opportunity of befriending genius ; thefe, to feize every opportunity of befriending themfelves, and, upon no account, to

H 2 harbour

harbour the moſt diſtant idea of quitting
the world, however it may be unworthy,
of them, leſt deſpondency ſhould at laſt
deceive them into ſo unpardonable a ſtep.
Chatterton, as appears by the Coroner's
Inqueſt, ſwallowed arſenick in water, on
the 24th of Auguſt 1770, and died in conſequence thereof the next day. He was
buried in a ſhell, in the burying ground
of Shoe-lane work-houſe *." Whatever
unfiniſhed pieces he might have, he cau-
tiouſly deſtroyed them before his death;
and his room, when broken open, was
found covered with little ſcraps of paper †. What muſt increaſe our regret
for this haſty and unhappy ſtep, is the information that the late Dr. Fry, head of
St. John's College in Oxford, went to
Briſtol in the latter end of Auguſt 1770,
in order to ſearch into the hiſtory of Rowley and Chatterton, and to patroniſe the
latter,

* Love and Madneſs, p. 221.
† Ibid. p. 222.

latter, if he appeared to deferve affiftance—
when, alas! all the intelligence he could
procure was, that Chatterton had, within
a few days, deftroyed himfelf *.

I have been induced, from the circum-
ftances of the narrative, repeatedly to confider the character of Chatterton in the
different ftages of life in which I had occafion to contemplate him. Indeed, the
character of any man is better underftood
from a fair and accurate ftatement of his
life and conduct, than from the comments
of any critic or biographer whatever. A
few general obfervations, which could not
with fo much propriety be introduced into
the body of the narrative, I fhall, however, venture to fubjoin; though I flatter
myfelf the reader is not at this time unac-
quainted with the outline of his moral portrait.

The perfon of Chatterton, like his
genius, was premature; he had a man-

H 3

linefs.

* Love and Madnefs, p, 226.

linefs and dignity beyond his years, and
there was a fomething about him uncommonly prepoffeffing. His moft remarkable feature was his eyes; which,
though gray, were uncommonly pierc-
ing; when he was warmed in argument,
or otherwife, they fparked with fire, and
one eye, it is faid, was ftill more remarkable than the other*. His genius
will be moft completely eftimated from his
writings. He had an uncommon ardour
in the purfuit of knowledge, and uncommon facility in the attainment of it. It
was a favourite maxim with him, that
" man is equal to any thing, and that
every thing might be atchieved by diligence and abftinence †." His imagination,

* Love and Madnefs, p. 271.

† Ibid. p. 183. If any uncommon character was mentioned in his hearing, ": All boy as he was, he would only
obferve, that the perfon in queftion merited praife; but
that God had fent his creatures into the world with arms
long enough to reach any thing, if they would be at the
trouble of extending them." Ib.

tion, like Dryden's, was more fertile than correct; and he seems to have erred rather through haste and negligence, than through any deficiency of taste. He was above that puerile affectation which pretends to borrow nothing; he knew that original genius confists in forming new and happy combinations, rather than in searching after thoughts and ideas which never had occurred before; and that the man who never imitated, has seldom acquired a habit of good writing. If those poems, which pass under the name of Rowley, be really the productions of Chatterton, he possessed the strongest marks of a vigorous imagination and a sound judgment, in forming great, confiftent, and ingenious plots, and making choice of the most interesting subjects. If Rowley and Chatterton be the same, it will be difficult to say whether he excelled moft in the sublime or the satirical; and as a universal genius, he must rank

above

above Dryden, and perhaps only stand second to Shakespeare. If, on the other hand,
we are to judge altogether from those pieces
which are confessedly his own, we must
undoubtedly assign the preference to those
of the satirical class. In most of his serious writings, there is little that indicates
their being composed with a full relish;
when he is satirical, his soul glows in his
composition.

Mr. Catcott affirms that Chatterton un-
derstood no language but his mother
tongue; the same fact seems to be implied
in his own confession, " that he spoke no
tongue but his own *;" and it receives decisive confirmation from the testimony of
Mr. Smith, in his conversation with Dr.
Glynn; yet we find him, even so early
as the year 1768, annexing a Latin signature to the " Accounte of the Fryers
passing

---

* Love and Madness, p. 198.

paffing the old Bridge," and there are
fome attempts at infcriptions in old French,
in the defign which he planned for his
own tomb-ftone *. He, probably, might
have acquired fome little knowledge of
both thefe languages; but even if this
were the cafe, there can be no doubt that
it was very fuperficial. When we confider the variety of his engagements while
at Briftol, his extenfive reading, and the
great knowledge he had acquired of the
ancient language of his native country, we
cannot wonder that he had not time to
occupy himfelf in the ftudy of other languages; and after his arrival in London,
he had a new and neceffary fcience to learn,
the world; and that he made the moft advantageous ufe of his time is evident from
the extenfive knowledge of mankind difplayed in the different effays, which he
produced occafionally for periodical publications.

* Chatterton's Will, in App. to Mifc.

cations. The lively and vigorous imagination of Chatterton contributed, doubtlefs, to animate him with that fpirit of enterprife, which led him to form fo many impracticable and vifionary fchemes, for the acquifition of fame and fortune. His ambition was evident from his earlieft youth; and perhaps the inequality of his fpirits might, in a great meafure, depend upon the fairnefs of his views, or the diffipation of his projects. His melancholy was extreme on fome occafions, and, at thofe times, he conftantly argued in favour of fuicide. Mr. Catcott left him one evening totally deprefied; but he returned the next morning with unufual fpirits. He faid, "he had fprung a mine," and produced a parchment, containing the *Sprytes*, a poem, now in the poffeffion of Mr. Barrett *.

His

* From the information of Mr. Seward.

His natural melancholy was not corrected by the irreligious principles, which he
had so unfortunately imbibed. To these
we are certainly to attribute his premature
death; and, if he can be proved guilty of
the licentiousness which is by some laid to
his charge, it is reasonable to believe that
a system, which exonerates the mind from
the apprehension of future punishment,
would not contribute much to restrain the
criminal excesses of the passions. Had
Chatterton lived, and been fortunate enough
to fall into settled and sober habits of life,
his excellent understanding would, in all
probability, have led him to see the fallacy
of those principles, which he had hastily
embraced; as it was, the only preserva-
tives of which he was possessed against the
contagion of vice, were the enthusiasm of
literature, and that delicacy of sentiment
which taste and reading inspire. But
[though these auxiliaries are not wholly to
be

despised, we have too many instances of their inefficacy in supporting the cause of virtue, to place any confident reliance on them.

Under such circumstances there is little cause for surprize, if the passions of Chatterton should frequently have trespassed the boundaries of reason and moral duty. That he had strong resentments is evident from his great disposition to satire, and particularly from the letter which has been mentioned as written by him to his schoolmaster, soon after the commencement of his apprenticeship. That he was "proud and imperious," is allowed by his sister, and the generality of his acquaintance. He stands charged with a profligate attachment to women; the accusation, however, is stated in a vague and desultory manner, as if from common report, without any direct or decided evidence in support of the opinion. To the regula-

rity

rity of his conduct during his residence in
Bristol, some respectable testimonies have
been already exhibited. It is, indeed, by
no means improbable, that a young man
of strong passions, and unprotected by religious principles, might frequently be
unprepared to resist the temptations of a
licentious metropolis; yet, even after his
arrival in London, there are some proofs in
his favour, which ought not to be disre-
garded. During a residence of nine weeks
at Mr. Walmsley's, he never staid out beyond the family hours, except one night,
when Mrs. Ballance knew that he lodged
at the house of a relation*.

Whatever may be the truth of these
reports, the list of his virtues still appears
to exceed the catalogue of his faults. His
temperance was in some respects exem-
plary. He seldom eat animal food, and
never tasted any strong or spirituous li-
quors:

* Love and Madness, p. 261.

quors: he lived chiefly on a morſel of bread or a tart, with a draught of water. His ſiſter affirms, that he was a lover of truth from the earlieſt dawn of reaſon; and that his ſchool-maſter depended on his veracity on all occaſions *: the pride of genius will ſeldom deſcend to the moſt contemptible of vices, falſehood. His high ſenſe of dignity has been already noticed in two moſt ſtriking inſtances; but the moſt amiable feature in his character, was his generoſity and attachment to his mother and relations. Every favourite project for his advancement in life was accompanied with promiſes and encouragement to them; while in London, he continued to ſend them preſents, at a time when he was known himſelf to be in want: and indeed, the unremitting attention, kindneſs and reſpect, which appear in the whole of his conduct towards them, are deſerving the imitation of thoſe

der

* Mrs. N's letter, ibid.

in more fortunate circumſtances, and under the influence of better principles of
faith than Chatterton poſſeſſed *.

He had a number of friends, and notwithſtanding his diſpoſition to ſatire, he
is ſcarcely known to have had any enemies. By the accounts of all who were
acquainted with him, there was ſomething uncommonly inſinuating in his
manner and converſation. Mr. Crofs informed Mr. Warton, that in Chatterton's frequent viſits while he reſided at
Brook-ſtreet, he found his converſation,
a little infidelity excepted, moſt captivat-
ing †. His extenſive, though in many inſtances, ſuperficial knowledge, united with
his genius, wit and fluency, muſt have
admirably accompliſhed him for the plea-
ſures of ſociety. His pride, which perhaps

* It can never be ſufficiently lamented, that this amiable
propenſity was not more uniform in Chatterton. A real
love for his relations ought to have arreſted the hand of
ſuicide ; but when religion is loſt, all uniformity of prin-
ciple is loſt. O.
† Warton's Inquiry, 107.

haps, fhould rather be termed the ftrong confcioufnefs of intellectual excellence, did not deftroy his affability. He was always acceffible, and rather forward to make acquaintance, than apt to decline the advances of others*. There is reafon, however to believe, that the inequality of his fpirits, affected greatly his behaviour in company. His fits of abfence were frequent and long. "He would often look ftedfaftly in a perfon's face without fpeaking, or feeming to fee the perfon, for a quarter of an hour or more.†."

Chatterton had one ruling paffion which governed his whole conduct, and that was the defire of literary fame; this paffion intruded itself on every occafion, and abforbed his whole attention. Whether he would have

---

* "Laft week being in the pit of Drury Lane theatre, "I contracted an immediate acquaintance (which you know "is no hard tafk to me) with a young gentleman, &c. Letter to his mother, Love and Madnefs, p. 197.

† Love and Madnefs, p. 214.

have continued to improve or the contrary, must have depended in some measure on the circumstances of his future life. Had he fallen into profligate habits and connections, he would probably have lost a great part of his ardour for the cultivation of his mind; and his maturer age would only have diminished the admiration which the efforts of his childhood have so justly excited.

At the shrine of Chatterton, some grateful incense has been offered. Mr. Warton speaks of him as "a prodigy of genius," as, "a singular instance of a prematurity of abilities." He adds, that "he possessed a comprehension of mind, and an activity of understanding, which predominated over his situation in life, and his opportunities of instruction*." And Mr. Malone "believes him to have been the greatest genius that England has produced

I

* History of English poetry.

duced fince the days of Shakefpear*."
Mr. Croft†, the ingenious author of
Love and Madnefs, to whom in the
courfe of this work I have had many
obligations, is ftill more unqualified in his
praifes. He afferts, that "no fuch human
being, at any period of life, has ever been
known, or poffibly ever will be known."
He adds, in another place, "an army of
Macedonian and Swedifh mad butchers,
indeed, fly before him; nor does my memory fupply me with any human being,
who, at fuch an age, with fuch difadvantages, has produced fuch compofitions ‡.

Under

---

* Curfory Obfervations on the Poems attributed to Rowley, p. 41.

† Editor of an intended new Englifh Dictionary.

‡ *Mohammed*, it is true, with hardly the ufual education of
his illiterate tribe, unable (as was imagined, and he pretended) even to read or write, *forged* the KORAN ; which
is to this day the moft elegant compofition in the Arabic
language, and its ftandard of excellence. Upon the argument of improbability, that a man fo illiterate fhould compofe a book fo admired, *Mohammed* artfully refted the prin-
ciptal

Under the Heathen mythology, superstition and admiration would have explained all by bringing Apollo upon
earth: nor would the god ever have
descended with more credit to himself."

The following parallel also by the
same ingenious critic, does equal credit
to the ingenuity of its author, and the
reputation of Chatterton.

Milton enjoyed every ad-	Chatterton wanted every.
vantage not only of private,	advantage of every possible
but of public, not only of	education.
domestic, but of foreign edu-	
cation,	
Milton	Chatterton

cipal evidence of his *Koran's* divinity. (Sale's Koran,
P. Discourse, p. 42, 60.) He, who, merely from improbability, denies Chatterton to be the author of Rowley's
Poems, must go near to admit God to be the author of the
Koran. But, before we compare together Chatterton and
Mohammed, it should be remembered that Mohammed was
forty when he commenced prophet. Perhaps the most extraordinary circumstance about Mohammed is, that even
familiarity could not sink him into contempt; that he
contrived to be a hero and a prophet, even to his wives and
his *valets de chambre*. Even his fits of the epilepsy he converted into proofs of his divine mission. It is probable,
that, if *Mohammed* had been less salacious, and not subject

to

Milton in his youth received such instructions from teachers and schoolmasters, that, in his age, he was able to become a schoolmaster, and a teacher to others.

Milton's juvenile writings would not have justified a prophecy of Paradise Loft: but the author of them flatters himself, by dating his life 15 till he had turned 16.

Milton did not produce *Comus* much earlier than in his 26th year; since it was first presented at Ludlow in 1634, and he was born in 1608. In 1645, when he was 37, Allegro and Penserofo, first appeared. In 1655, when he was 47, after *long choosing, and beginning late,* he set himself to turn a strange thing, called a Mystery, into an epic poem; which was not completed in less than Chatterton's whole active existence, since the copy was not sold till April, 1667,

Chatterton became his own teacher and his own schoolmaster before other children are subjects for instruction; and never knew any other.

Few, if any, of Milton's juvenile writings would have been owned by Chatterton, at least by Rowley, could he have paft for the author of them.

Chatterton, not suffered to be *long choosing,* or to *begin late,* in 17 years and 9 months, reckoning from his cradle to his grave, produced the volume of Rowley's poems, his volume of Miscellanies, and many things which are not printed, beside what his indignation tore in pieces the day he spurned at the world, and threw himself on the anger of his Creator.

to the falling sickness, out of thirty equal divisions of the known world, whereof Christianity claims five, and Paganism nineteen, the inhabitants of six would not now believe in the *Koran.*

1667, and then confifted only of 10 books. With all its glorious perfections, Paradife Loft contains puerilities, to which Chatterton was a ftranger. In 3 years more, when he was 62, appeared Milton's Hiftory of England, Paradife Regained, and Sampfon, were publifhed in the fame year. Lycidas, I had forgotten. It was written in his 29th year. That propriety of character and fituation, which Chatterton can feldom have violated, or he would not to this moment deceive fuch and fo many men, Milton feldom preferves in Lycidas. If, in the courfe of an exiftence almoft four times longer than Chatterton's, this man *(fallen on evil days and evil tongues,* with lefs truth than Chatterton), who bore no fruit worth gathering till after the age at which Chatterton was withered by the hand of Death—if, I fay, this great man produced other writings, he will not quarrel that pofterity has forgotten them; if he fhould, pofterity will ftill perhaps forget them.

Milton's manuscripts, preserved at Cambridge, bear testimony to his frequent and commendable correction.

Milton, as Ellwood relates, could never bear to hear Paradise Lost preferred before Paradise Regained. He is known to have pronounced Dryden to be no poet.

Milton, more from inclination than want of bread, it seems, entered into party disputes, whether a king might be lawfully beheaded, &c. with a servility and a virulence, and let out his praise to hire, perhaps, with a meanness, at all periods of his life, which the worst enemies of Chatterton cannot prove him to have equalled.

Milton, in affluence (if compared with others beside Chatterton)

What time could Chatterton have found for alteration or correction, when I maintain that any boy who should only have fairly *transcribed*, before his 18th year, all that Chatterton, before his 18th year, invented and composed, would be thought to deserve the reputation of diligence, and the praise of application?

If Chatterton, much earlier in life than Milton was calculated either to be an author or a critick, had not possessed a chaster judgment, he would not still impose on so many criticks and authors.

Chatterton, in order to procure bread for himself, a grandmother, mother and sister, was ready to prove the patriotism of Bute, or of Beckford, in writings, which older men need not blush to own, and in an age when older men did not blush at such a *profession*.

Chatterton, steeped to the lips in poverty, entertained, long

Chatterton) felt on his brows those laurels which others could not see; and was perfuaded that, "by labour and intenfe ftudy, his portion in this life, he might leave fomething fo written to after-times, as they fhould not willingly let it die."

Paradife Loft produced the author and the widow only 28 pounds. The meaner, more fervile, and more verfatile abilities of the author produced him indeed enough to be deprived of four thoufand pounds by ill-fortune, and to leave fifteen hundred pounds to his family.

Phillips relates of Milton, from his own mouth, that "his vein never happily flowed but from the autumnal equinox to the vernal." Richardfon writes, that "his poetical faculty would on a fudden rufh upon him with an impetus or æftrum."

Milton, when a man, feldom drank any thing ftrong: he ate with delicacy and temperance.

long before he had lived 18 years, ideas, hopes, perfuafions, *(by labour and intenfe ftudy,* more truly *his portion in this life* than Milton's) of living to all eternity in the memory of Fame.

Mr. Catcott and Mr. Barreit muft inform the world whether Rowley's poems **and** his own together produced Chattertòn 28 fhillings.

What is faid of Chattertòn, and of the moon's effect upon him, you have read.

Chatterton, when a boy, hardly ever touched meat, and drank only water: when a child, he would often refufe

...... fuse to take any thing but
bread and water, even if it
did happen that his mother
had a hot meal, "because
" he had a work in hand,
" and he must not make
" himself more stupid, than
" God had made him."

Milton's historians and
grand-daughter admit his
morosenefs to his children,
and that he would not let
them learn to write.

Chatterton's mother, his
sister and his letters, can
speak best of his heart, and
of his wishes that his sister
might learn every thing.

To these I shall add the testimony of
Mr. Knox:

" Unfortunate boy! short and evil were
thy days, but thy fame shall be immortal.
Hadst thou been known to the munificent
patrons of genius—

" Unfortunate boy! poorly wast thou
accommodated during thy short sojourning
among us;—rudely wast thou treated,—
forely did thy feeling foul suffer from the
scorn of the unworthy; and there are, at

last,

laft, thofe who wifh to rob thee of thy
only meed, thy pofthumous glory. Severe too are the cenfurers of thy morals.
In the gloomy moments of defpondency,
I fear thou haft uttered impious and blaf-
phemous thoughts, which none can defend, and which neither thy youth, nor
thy fiery fpirit, nor thy fituation, can excufe. But let thy more rigid cenfors reflect, that thou waft literally and ftrictly
but a boy. Let many of thy bitterest
enemies reflect what were their own religious principles, and whether they had
any, at the age of fourteen, fifteen, and
fixteen. Surely it is a fevere and an un-
juft furmife, that thou wouldeft probably
have ended thy life as a victim of the
laws, if thou hadft not finifhed it as thou
didft; fince the very act by which thou
durft put an end to thy painful exiftence,
proves that thou thoughteft it better to
die,

die, than to support life by theft or violence.

"The speculative errors of a boy who
wrote from the sudden suggestions of paffion or despondency, who is not convicted
of any immoral or dishoneft act in confequence of his speculations, ought to be
configned to oblivion. But there feems
to be a general and inveterate diflike to
the boy, exclusively of the poet; a diflike which many will be ready to impute,
and, indeed, not without the appearance
of reafon, to that infolence and envy of
the little great, which cannot bear to ac-
knowledge fo tranfcendent and command-
ing a fuperiority in the humble child of
want and obfcurity.

"Malice, if there was any, may furely
now be at reft; for "Cold he lies in the
grave below." But where were ye, O ye
friends to genius, when, ftung with dif-
appointment,

appointment, diftreffed for food and rai-
ment, with every frightful form of human mifery painted on his fine imagination, poor Chatterton funk in defpair?
Alas! ye knew him not then, and now it
is to late,—

> For now he is dead;
> Gone to his death bed,
> All under the willow tree.

So fang the fweet youth, in as tender
an elegy as ever flowed from a feeling
heart.

" In return for the pleafure I have received from thy poems, I pay thee, poor
boy, the trifling tribute of my praife.
Thyfelf thou haft emblazoned; thine
own monument thou haft erected: But
they whom thou haft delighted, feel a
pleafure in vindicating thine honours
from the rude attacks of detrac-
tion *".

The

* Knox's Effays, No. 144.

The poetic eulogiums have, however, exceeded, both in number and excellence, the compliments of critical writers; a few remarkably interefting and beautiful, I fhall felect, with the double view of adorning the work, and gratifying the reader.

A poet, whofe fuperior elegance and claffical tafte do not appear to have met with all the applaufe they have deferved, thus fpeaks of Chatterton:

" Yet as with ftreaming eye the forrowing mufe,
" Pale CHATTERTON's untimely urn bedews;
" Her accents fhall arraign the partial care,
" That fhielded not her fon from cold defpair.*

There is a beautiful monody written by Mrs. Cowley, inferted in the laft edition of Love and Madnefs.—It is as follows:

O CHATTERTON! for thee the penfive fong I raife,
Thou object of my wonder, pity, envy, praife!
Bright Star of Genius!—torn from life and fame,
My tears, my verfe, fhall confecrate thy name!

Ye

* Pye's Progrefs of Refinement, Part 2.

Ye Mufes! who around his natal bed
Triumphant fung, and all your influence fhed;
APOLLO! thou who rapt his infant breaft,
And in his dædal numbers fhone confeft,
Ah! why, in vain, fuch mighty gifts beftow?
—Why give frefh tortures to the Child of Woe?
Why thus, with barb'rous care, illume his mind,
Adding new fenfe to all the ills behind?

Thou haggard Poverty! whofe cheerlefs eye
Transforms young Rapture to the pond'rous figh,
In whofe drear cave no Mufe e'er ftruck the lyre,
Nor Bard e'er madden'd with poetic fire;
Why all thy fpells for CHATTERTON combine?
His thought creative, why muft thou confine?
Subdu'd by thee, his pen no more obeys,
No longer gives the fong of ancient days;
Nor paints in glowing tints from diftant fkies,
Nor bids wild fcen'ry rufh upon our eyes——
Check'd in her flight, his rapid Genius cowers,
Drops her fad plumes, and yields to thee her powers.

Behold him, Mufes! fee your fav'rite fon
The prey of want, ere manhood is begun!
The bofom ye have fill'd, with anguifh torn——
The mind you cherifh'd, drooping and forlorn!

And now Defpair her fable form extends,
Creeps to his couch, and o'er his pillow bends,
Ah, fee! a deadly bowl the fiend conceal'd,
Which to his eye with caution is reveal'd——
Seize it, Apollo!—feize the liquid fnare!
Dafh it to earth, or diffipate in air!
Stay, haplefs Youth! refrain—abhor the draught,
With pangs, with racks, with deep repentance fraught!

Oh,

Oh, hold! the cup with woe ETERNAL flows,
More—more than Death the pois'nous juice beſtows!
In vain!—he drinks—and now the ſearching fires
Ruſh through his veins, and writhing he expires!
No ſorrowing friend, no ſiſter, parent, nigh,
To ſooth his pangs, or catch his parting ſigh ;
Alone, unknown, the Muſe's darling dies,
And with the vulgar dead unnoted lies!
Bright Star of Genius !—torn from life and fame,
My tears, my verſe, ſhall conſecrate thy name!

Nor has the Muſe of Amwell been backward in commendation.

And BRISTOL! why thy ſcenes explore,
    And why thoſe ſcenes ſo ſoon reſign,
And fail to ſeek the ſpot that bore
    That wonderous tuneful Youth of thine,
The Bard, whoſe boaſted ancient ſtore
Roſe recent from his own exhauſtleſs mine † !

Though Fortune all her gifts denied,
    Though Learning made him not her choice,
The Muſe ſtill placed him at her ſide,
    And bade him in her ſmile rejoice—
Deſcription ſtill his pen ſupplied,
Pathos his thought, and Melody his voice!

Conſcious and proud of merit high,
    Fame's wreath he boldly claim'd to wear ;

But

---

† This is at leaſt the Author's opinion, notwithſtanding all that has
hitherto appeared on the other ſide of the queſtion. The laſt line
alludes to one of the ingenious Mr. Maſon in his Elegy to a young
Nobleman :

    " See from the depths of his exhauſtleſs mine
    " His glittering ſtores the tuneful ſpendthrift throws."

But Fame, regardless, pass'd him by,
   Unkhown, or deem'd unworth her care:
  The Sun of Hope forsook his sky;
And all his land look'd dreary, bleak, and bare!

  Then Poverty, grim spectre, rose,
   And horror o'er the prospect threw—
His deep distress too nice to expose;
  Too nice for common aid to sue,
  A dire alternative he chose,
And rashly from the painful scene withdrew.

  Ah! why for Genius' headstrong rage
   Did Virtue's hand no curb prepare?
What boots, poor youth! that now thy page
  Can boast the public praise to share,
The learn'd in deep research engage,
And lightly entertain the gentle fair?

  Ye, who superfluous wealth command,
   O why your kind relief delay'd?
O why not snatch'd his desperate hand?
  His foot on Fate's dread brink not stay'd?
What thanks had you your native land
For a new SHAKESPEARE or new MILTON paid!

  For me—Imagination's power
   Leads oft insensibly my way,
To where, at midnight's silent hour,
  The crescent moon's slow-westering ray
Pours full on REDCLIFF's lofty tower,
And gilds with yellow light its walls of grey.

  'Midst Toil and Commerce slumbering round,
   Lull'd by the rising tide's hoarse roar,
There Frome and Avon willow-crown'd,
  I view sad-wandering by the shore,

With

With ftreaming tears, and notes of mournful found,
Too late their haplefs Bard, untimely loft, deplore.

The following lines are uncommonly
animated and poetical:

If changing times fuggeft the pleafing hope,
That Bards no more with adverfe fortune cope;
That in this alter'd clime, where Arts increafe,
And make our polifh'd Ifle a fecond Greece;
That now, if Poefy proclaims her Son,
And challenges the wreath by Fancy won;
Both Fame and Wealth adopt him as their heir,
And liberal Grandeur makes his life her care;
From fuch vain thoughts thy erring mind defend,
And look on CHATTERTON's difaftrous end.
Oh, ill-ftarr'd Youth, whom Nature form'd in vain,
With powers on Pindus' fplendid height to reign!
O dread example of what pangs await
Young Genius ftruggling with malignant fate!
What could the Mufe, who fir'd thy infant frame
With the rich promife of Poetic fame;
Who taught thy hand its magic art to hide,
And mock the infolence of Critic pride;
What cou'd her unavailing cares oppofe,
To fave her darling from his defperate foes;
From preffing Want's calamitous controul,
And Pride, the fever of the ardent foul?
Ah, fee, too confcious of her failing power,
She quits her Nurfling in his deathful hour!
In a chill room, within whofe wretched wall
No cheering voice replies to Mifery's call;
Near a vile bed, too crazy to fuftain
Misfortune's wafted limbs, convuls'd with pain,

On

On the bare floor, with heaven-directed eyes,
The hapless Youth in speechless horror lies!
The pois'nous phial, by distraction drain'd,
Rolls from his hand, in wild contortion strain'd:
Pale with life-wasting pangs, it's dire effect,
And stung to madness by the world's neglect,
He, in abhorrence of the dangerous Art,
Once the dear idol of his glowing heart,
Tears from his Harp the vain detested wires,
And in the frenzy of Despair expires * !

Again, with all the honest resentment of indignant Genius,

Search the dark scenes were drooping Genius lies,
And keep from sorriest sights a nation's eyes,
That, from expiring Want's reproaches free,
Our generous country ne'er may weep to see
A future CHATTERTON by poison dead,
An OTWAY fainting for a little bread † .

To these elegant offerings to the genius of Chatterton, it is with peculiar plea-sure I add a sonnet to expression, from the polished and pathetic pen of Miss Helen Maria Williams.

Expression, child of soul! I fondly trace
Thy strong enchantments, when the poet's lyre,
The painter's pencil catch thy sacred fire,
And beauty wakes for thee her touching grace—
But from this frighted glance thy form avert
When horrors check thy tear, thy struggling sigh,
When frenzy rolls in thy impassion'd eye,
Or guilt sits heavy on thy lab'ring heart—

K

Nor

* Hayley's Essay on Epic Poetry, Ep. iv. l. 211 to 248.
† Ibid. 226 to 242.

Nor ever let my fhudd'ring fancy bear
  The wafting groan, or view the pallid look
  Of him * the Mufes lov'd—when hope forfook
His fpirit, vainly to the Mufes dear !
For charm'd with heav'nly fong, this bleeding breaft,
Mourns the bleft power of verfe could give defpair no
  reft.—

Independent of the poems attributed to
Rowley, Chatterton has left behind him
a variety of pieces, publifhed and unpub-
lifhed ; the moft confiderable of the former are to be found in a volume of mifcellanies, publifhed in 1778, to which is
prefixed a fketch for the late Alderman
Beckford's ftatue, a fpecimen of Chatterton's abilities in the arts of drawing and
defign ; and this publication was followed
in 1786, by " a fuppliment to the mifcellanies of Thomas Chatterton." The compofitions contained in both thefe volumes,
are fcarcely to be infpected with all the
feverity of criticifm. Confiderable allow-
ances ought to be made for the exercifes
                              of

* Chatterton.

of his infantine years, for the incorrect effusions of momentary resentment, for a few lines thrown together in a playful mood to please an illiterate female, or to amuse a school-fellow, and perhaps not less for the hasty and involuntary productions of indigence and necessity, constructed for a magazine, and calculated for the sole purpose of procuring a subsistence. Of the poetical part of these miscellanies, I have already intimated, that the serious are inferior to the satirical.

In the elegy to the memory of Mr. Thomas Phillips, of Fairford, we, however, meet with some descriptive stanzas, perhaps not unworthy the author of Rowley's poems:

" Pale rugged Winter bending o'er his head,
" His grizzled hair bedropt with icy dew;
" His eyes, a dusky light, congealed and dead;
" His robe, a tinge of bright ethereal blue.
" His train a motley'd, sanguine sable cloud,
" He limps along the russet dreary moor;
" Whilst rising whirlwinds, blasting, keen and loud,
" Roll the white surges to the sounding shore."

" Fancy,

" Fancy, whose various, figure-tinctured veſt
" Was ever changing to a different hue;
" Her head, with varied bays and flow'rets, dreſt,
" Her eyes two ſpangles of the morning dew."

" Now as the mantle of the evening ſwells,
" Upon my mind I feel a thick'ning gloom!
" Ah! could I charm, by friendſhip's potent ſpells,
" The ſoul of Philip's from the deathy tomb!
" Then would we wander thro' the dark'ned vale,
" In converſe ſuch as heavenly ſpirits uſe,
" And borne upon the plumage of the gale,
" Hymn the creator and exhort the Muſe*."

In a letter to his friend Cary, dated
London, July 1, 1770, Chatterton tells
him, " in the laſt London magazine, and
in that which comes out to day, are the
only two pieces of mine I have the vanity
to call poetry." Theſe were the two
African Eclogues, publiſhed in his Miſcellanies. I am ſorry I cannot unite with
the author in the commendation of theſe
pieces; but Chatterton, as well as Milton, ſeems to have been incapable of eſti-
mating rightly the reſpective merits of his
　　　　　　　　　　　　　　　　own

* Chatterton's Miſcellanies.

own productions *. They are, uncon-
nected and unequal, though it must be
confessed, that they contain some excellent lines; the following occur almost at
the beginning of the first eclogue, and are
animated, expressive and harmonious:

" High from the ground the youthful warriors sprung,
" Loud on the concave shell the lances rung:
" In all the mystic mazes of the dance,
" The youths of Banny's burning sands advance,
" Whilst the soft virgin, panting, looks behind,
" And rides upon the pinions of the wind †."

Of the correctness of the following
simile in the second eclogue, I shall not
determine; but the liveliness of the description evinces a most vigorous imagination.

" On Tiber's banks, close rank'd, a warring train,
" Stretch'd to the distant edge of Galca's plain:
" So when arrived at Gaigra's highest steep,
" We view the wide expansion of the deep;
" See in the gilding of her wat'ry robe,
" The quick declension of the circling globe;

K 3

" From

---

* I know some respectable friends, who esteem this instance of bad
taste, as a strong presumptive argument against Chatterton being the author of Rowley's poems.
† Chatterton's Miscellanies, p. 56.

" From the blue sea a chain of mountains rise,
" Blended at once with water and with skies :
" Beyond our sight in vast extension curl'd,
" The check of waves, the guardian of the world *."

The satire of Chatterton has more of the luxuriance, fluency, and negligence of Dryden, than of the terseness and refinement of Pope. The following lines are in the style of the former:

" Search nature o'er, procure me, if you can,
" The fancied character, an honest man.
" A man of sense not honest by constraint,
" (For fools are canvass, living but in paint)
" To Mammon, or to superstition slaves,
" All orders of mankind are fools or knaves :
" In the first attribute by none surpass'd,
" * * * * endeavours to obtain the last †."

The following is an evident imitation of Mr. Pope, even to the cadence of the verse; but it is not equally successful with the last specimen;

" But why must Chatterton selected sit,
" The butt of every Critic's little wit ?
" Am I alone for ever in a crime,
" *Nonsense in prose, or blasphemy in rhyme?*

" All

* Chatterton's Miscellanies, p. 56.
† Epistle to the Rev. Mr. Catcott, Append. to Chat. Misc. p. 25.

" All monofyllables a line appears !—
" Is it not very often fo in Shears ?
" See gen'rous Eccas, length'ning out my praife,
" Inraptured with the mufic of my lays;
" In all the arts of panegyric grac'd,
" The cream of modern literary tafte *."

In a poem on Happinefs, inferted in
Love and Madnefs, are fome ftrokes of
fatire in a fuperior ftyle:

" Come to my pen, companion of the lay,
" And fpeak of worth, where merit ————
" Let lazy B——— undiftinguifh'd fnore,
" Nor lafh his generofity to ———,
" Praife him for fermons of his curate bought,
" His eafy flow of words, his depth of thought ;
" His active fpirit ever in difplay,
" His great devotion when he drawls to pray,
" His fainted foul diftinguifhably feen,
" With all the virtues of a modern Dean †."

" Pulvis, whofe knowledge centres in degrees,
" Is never happy but when taking fees:
" Bleft with a bufhy wig and folemn pace,
" Catcott admires him for a *foffile* face."
—" Mould'ring in duft the fair Lavinia lies,
" Death and our Doctor clos'd her fparkling eyes,
" O all ye pow'rs, the guardians of the world !
" Where is the ufelefs bolt of vengeance hurl'd ?

K 4   " Say |

* The Defence, ibid. p. 37.
† Love and Madnefs, p. 155.

"Say, shall this leaden sword of plague prevail,
"And kill the mighty where the mighty fail?
"Let the red bolus tremble o'er his head,
"And with his guardian julep strike him dead *!"

In the volume of his miscellanies are two political pieces, the Consuliad, written at Bristol, and in the highest strain of party scurrility †; and the Prophecy, written apparently a short time after, which is in the best style of Swift's minor

* Love and Madness, 156.

† The introduction to this poem is not destitute of merit.

Of warring senators, and battles dire,
Of quails uneaten; Muse, awake the lyre.
Where C—pb—ll's chimneys overlook the square,
And N—t—n's future prospects hang in air;
Where counsellors dispute, and cockers match,
And Caledonian earls in concert scratch;
A group of heroes, occupied the round,
Long in the rolls of infamy renown'd.
Circling the table all in silence sat,
Now 'tearing bloody lean, now champing fat;
Now picking ortolans, and chicken slain,
To form the whimsies of an *à-la-reine*:
Now storming castles of the newest taste,
And granting articles to forts of paste:
Now swallowing bitter draughts of Prussian beer;
Now sucking tallow of salubrious deer.

nor pieces, and appears to be the genuine effusion of that enthusiastic love of liberty, which in tumultuous times generally takes possession of young and sanguine dispositions.* Of

* THE PROPHECY.

This truth of old was sorrow's friend,
" Times at the worst will surely mend."
The difficulty's then to know,
How long oppression's clock can go;
When Britain's sons may cease to sigh,
And hope that their redemption's nigh.

When Vice exalted takes the lead,
And Vengeance hangs but by a thread;
Gay peeresses turn'd out o'doors;
Whoremasters peers, and sons of whores;
Look up, ye Britons! cease to sigh,
For your redemption draweth nigh.

When vile Corruption's brazen face,
At council-board shall take her place;
And lords-commissioners resort,
To welcome her at Britain's court;
Look up, ye Briotns! cease to sigh,
For your redemption draweth nigh.

See Pension's harbour large and clear,
Defended by St. Stephen's pier!
The entrance safe, by Current led,
Tiding round G——'s jetty head;
Look up, ye Britons! cease to sigh,
For your redemption draweth nigh.

When

Of the profe compofitions of Chatterton,
his imitations of Offian are certainly the
worft : he has not indeed improved upon
. . . . an

When Civil-Power fhall fnore at eafe,
While foldiers fire—to keep the peace;
When murders fanctuary find,
And petticoats can Juftice blind ;
Look up, ye Britons! ceafe to figh,
For your redemption draweth nigh.

Commerce o'er Bondage will prevail,
Free as the wind, that fills her fail.
When fhe complains of vile reftraint,
And Power is deaf to her complaint ;
Look up, ye Britons ! ceafe to figh,
For your redemption draweth nigh.

When raw projectors fhall begin
Oppreffion's hedge, to keep her in ;
She in difdain will take her flight,
And bid the Gotham fools good night ;
Look up, ye Britons ! ceafe to figh,
For your redemption draweth nigh.

When tax is laid, to fave debate,
By prudent minifters of ftate ;
And, what the people did not give,
Is levied by prerogative ;
Look up, ye Britons ! ceafe to figh,
For your redemption draweth nigh.

When Popifh bifhops dare to claim
Authority, in George's name ;

By

an indifferent model. They are full of wild imagery and inconfiftent metaphor, with

By Treafon's hand fet up, in fpite
Of George's title, William's right;
Look up, ye Britons! ceafe to figh,
For your redemption draweth nigh.

When Popifh prieft a penfion draws
From ftarv'd exchequer, for the caufe
Commiffion'd, profelytes to make
In Britifh realms, for Britain's fake;
Look up, ye Britons! ceafe to figh,
For your redemption draweth nigh.

When fnug in power, fly recufants
Make laws for Britifh Proteftants;
And d——g William's Revolution,
As Juftices claim execution;
Look up, ye Britons! ceafe to figh,
For your redemption draweth nigh.

When foldiers, paid for our defence,
In wanton pride flay innocence;
Blood from the ground for vengeance reeks,
Till Heaven the inquifition makes;
Look up, ye Britons! ceafe to figh,
For your redemption draweth nigh.

When at Bute's feet poor Freedom lies,
Mark'd by the prieft for facrifice,
And doom'd a victim, for the fins
Of half the *outs*, and all the *ins*;
Look up, ye Britons! ceafe to figh,
For your redemption draweth nigh,

When

with little either of plot or of character
to recommend them. His lighter Essays, such as the adventures of a star, the memoirs of a sad dog,
the

When Stewards pass a *boot* account;
And credit for the grofs amount;
Then to replace exhaufted ftore,
Mortgage the land to borrow more;
Look up, ye Britons! ceafe to figh,
For your redemption draweth nigh.

When fcrutineers, for private ends,
Againft the vote declare their friends;
Or judge, as you ftand there alive,
That five is more than forty-five;
Look up, ye Britons! ceafe to figh,
For your redemption draweth nigh.

When George fhall condefcend to hear
The modeft fuit, the humble prayer;
A prince, to purpled pride unknown!
No favourites difgrace the throne!
Look up, ye Britons! figh no more,
For your redemption's at the door.

When time fhall bring your wifh about,
Or, feven-years leafe, *you fold*, is out;
No future contract to fulfil;
Your tenants holding at your will;
Raife up your heads! your right demand!
For your redemption's in your hand.

Then

the hunter of oddities, &c. display considerable knowledge of what is called the
town, and demonstrate the keenness of his
observation, and his quickness in acquiring any branch of knowledge, or in adapt-
ing himself to any situation. We are to
remember, however, that he had been long
conversant in this species of composition,
and that a considerable fund of reading in
magazines, reviews, &c. which Mr. Warton observes " form the *school of the people*," had prepared him well to exercise
the profession of a periodical writer. Antiquities, however, constituted his favorite study, and in them his genius always
appears to the greatest advantage; even the
most humorous of his pieces (Tony Sel-
wood's

Then is your time to strike the blow,
And let the *slaves* of Mammon know,
Britain's true sons A BRIBE can scorn,
And die as *free* as they were born.
VIRTUE again shall take her seat,
And your redemption stand compleat.

wood's letter *) derives its principal excellence from his knowledge of ancient customs.

In the volume of Miscellanies attributed to him, there are some pieces to which his title is not well ascertained. Some with the signature of Asaphides, are claimed by one Lockstone, a linen-draper, and a particular acquaintance of Chatterton; and the story of Maria Friendless, which Chatterton himself sent to the Town and Country Magazine, probably for the sake of obtaining an immediate and necessary supply of money, is almost a literal transcript of the letter of Misella in the Rambler.

If the reputation of Chatterton, however, rested solely on those works, which he acknowledged as his own, it would neither be so extensive as it is, nor probably

* Chatterton's Miscellanies, p. 209.

bably so permanent as it is likely to continue, Rowley's poems have deservedly immortalized the name of Chatterton, and the controversy which their publication excited, is the most curious and extraordinary controversy, which, since the days of Bentley has divided the literary world.

I have already noticed the manner in which these poems are said to have been discovered. The account which Chatterton himself gave of the supposed author is nearly as follows :

THOMAS ROWLEY was born at Norton Mal-seward in Somersetshire, and educated at the convent of St. Kenna, at Keynesham *. He was of the clerical profession, was confessor to the two Canynge's, Robert and William, about the latter end of the reign of Henry the VIth,

or

* Note prefixed to "Ballade of Charitie." Rowley's poems, p. 203.

or about the beginning of that of Edward IV.; and was at leaft connected with our lady's church in Briftol *; though he is elfewhere ftyled the "parifh prieft of St. John's, in the city of Briftol †." After the death of Mr. Robert Canynge, (who at his brother's defire, bequeathed Rowley 100 marks) he was employed by that brother, Mr. William, to travel through a confiderable part of England to collect drawings. Mr. Canynge was fo well fatisfied with his fuccefs, that he rewarded him with a purfe of two hundred pounds, and promifed him that he fhould never be in want. He continued afterwards the confidential friend of Canynge. He wrote a variety of poems, many of them addreffed to that extraordinary character. He firft lived in a houfe on the hill, and afterwards

* Memoirs of Sir W. Canynge, Chatterton's Mifcellanies, p. 122.

† Introduction to the Battle of Haftings, Rowley's poems, p. 21.

afterwards in one by the Tower *; he ſurvived his patron, and died at Weſtbury, in Glouceſterſhire †. Such is Chatterton's account; but it is only fair to mention, that the exiſtence of any ſuch perſon as Rowley, is totally denied by the diſputants on one ſide of the controverſy.

There can, however, be no doubt concerning the exiſtence of W. Canynge, the patron of Rowley, ſince it is atteſted by ſuch a number of contemporary hiſtorians, and his remains lie interred in the church of which he was the founder. He is called by Chatterton, Sir William Canynge. He was the younger ſon of a citizen of Briſtol, and in his youth afforded early prognoſtics of wiſdom and ability. He was of a handſome perſon, and married for love, without a fortune. Soon after his marriage, his father and

L   his

* Chatterton's Miſcellanies, p. 127 & 128.
† Rowley's Poems, p. 203.

his eldeft brother (who both loved money as much as he defpifed it) died, and left him large eftates in land and money, and his brother John dependent upon him, whom he placed in fuch an advantageous line of bufinefs, that he afterwards became Lord-Mayor of London.

This dawn of profperity was, however, foon clouded by the death of his wife; to whofe memory he afforded the moft affectionate teftimony, in rejecting the moft fplendid propofals for a fecond marriage. Of his native city he was Mayor five times; and in the year 1461, when Sir Baldwin Fulford was executed for treafon, Canynge being then Mayor, pleaded for the criminal in vain. When he was knighted does not appear; but in the year 1467, a fecond marriage being propofed by the King, between him and one of the Widdeville, (the Queen's) family, Sir William went into holy orders purpofely

purposely to avoid it; and was ordained
Acolythe by his friend Carpenter, Bishop
of Worcester, the 19th of September.
He was afterwards dean of the Collegiate
church of Westbury in Wilts; with his
usual munificence he rebuilt that college,
and died in the year 1474, with the universal character of learning and virtue. Among
the proofs of his munificence there still exist an alms-house or hospital, with a chapel, and the beautiful church of St. Mary
Redcliffe, in Bristol *. At a great ex-
pense he had collected a cabinet of curiosities †; his collection of manuscripts,
among which were copies of his own and
Rowley's poems, were deposited in a
room in Redcliffe church: of the actual
or pretended discovery of which I have
already treated. Such is Chatterton's
history of Canynge, in which, though

L 2   there

---

* Story of W. Canynge, Rowley's poems, Chatterton's
Miscellanies, p. 112 to 122.   † Ibid.

there are some facts, which are amply
confirmed, there are also several which
are disputed by those who deny the authenticity of Rowley's poems.

These poems, we have already seen,
were produced by Chatterton at different
times, who asserted that he had copied
them from the fragments of those ancient
parchments, which his father had procured from the Redcliffe chest; he could
never be prevailed upon to produce any
originals, except a few fragments, the
largest not more than eight inches long,
and four and a half wide. The writing
on these fragments was at least a tolerable imitation of ancient manuscript, and
the parchment or vellum had every mark
of age. The only poetical originals which
he produced were, the challenge to Lydgate, the song to Ella, and Lydgate's answer, all contained in one parchment; the
account of W. Canynge's feast; the epitaph

taph on Robert Canynge, and part of the story of W. Canynge; befides thefe there are fome profe compofitions, and a few drawings, ftill in the hands of Mr. Barrett *.

The poems attributed to Rowley were firft collected in an octavo volume, and publifhed by Mr. Tyrwhitt, the learned editor of Chaucer; a very fplendid edition was afterwards publifhed in quarto, by the late Dr. Milles, dean of Exeter, and prefident of the Society of Antiquaries, with a preliminary differtation, and notes tending to prove that they were really written by Rowley and others in the 15th century.

The

* A complete lift of the original parchments, which were given to Mr. Barret by Chatterton, and which he has now in his hands, was communicated by that gentleman to Dr. Milles, and is as follows:

The Song to Ella, with the challenge to Lydgate and the Anfwer.

The poetical merit of these pieces is considerable. The subjects are interesting, and infinite imagination is displayed in the construction of the plots or fables, in the

arrangement

Answer. This poem was sent by Mr. Barret to a friend, and is unfortunately lost.

Canynge's Feast, a Poem.

The first thirty-six lines of the Storie of William Canynge.

The following are Historical Prose Compositions.

1. The Yellow Roll, containing an account of the origin of coinage in England, and of the curiosities in Canynge's cabinet. This also was lent with the song to Ella, by Mr. Barret to a friend, and is lost.

2. The purple Roll, thirteen inches by ten, containing an account of particular Coins, and the second and third Sections of Turgotus's History of Bristol. N. B. The first Section above quoted is also extant in Chatterton's own hand, but the original does not appear.

3. Vita Burtoni; a parchment roll, about eight inches long, and four broad, very closely written; containing an account of Sir Simon de Burton, and his rebuilding Redclift church.

4. Knights Templars Church; a History of its foundation, &c.

5. St. Mary's Church of the Port; a History of it from its foundation, ending with the verses on Robert Canynge.

6. Roll of Bartholomew's Priory, with a List of the Priors.

7. An

arrangement of the incidents, and the delineation of the characters. The beauties of poetry are scattered through them with no sparing hand. The Lyric productions in particular, such as the chorus's in the Tragedies, abound with luxuriant description, most vivid imagery, and striking metaphors. Through the veil of ancient language a happy adaptation of words

7. An account of the Chapel and House of Calendaries; *with a drawing of the chapel, and underneath an explanation of it.*

8. Ella's Chapple. No drawing, except to the Kist of Ella, but there is an account of its foundation.

9. St. Mary Magdalen's Chapel. A drawing only.

10. Grey Friars Church. A drawing only.

11. Drawing of three monumental Inscriptions.

12. Ancient Monument and Rudhall; mere delineations.

13. Lesser and Greater St. John's: only a rude delineation.

14. Several Drawings of the Castle of Bristol.

15. Strong Hold of the Castle: a drawing and account of its foundation, by Robert Earl of Gloucester, and Site thereof.

16. Old Wall of Bristol; mere drawings.

17. Carne of Robert Curthofes Mynde in Castle steed: a drawing or figure, with the words *Carne*, &c. underneath. Miller's Rowley, page 438.

words is still apparent, and a style both
energetic and expressive. Contrary to almost all the poetical productions of the
times, when they are supposed to have
been composed, they are in general conspicuous for the harmony and elegance of
the verse. Indeed, some passages are inferior in none of the essentials of poetry,
to the most finished productions of modern times.

On the other hand, it must not be dif-
sembled that some (and many will think
no inconsiderable) part of the charm of
these poems may probably result from the
Gothic sublimity of the style. Whatever is vulgar in language is lost by time,
and a small degree of obscurity in an ancient author gives a latitude to the fancy
of the reader, who generally imagines
the style to be more forcible and expressive than perhaps it intrinsically is.
We gaze with wonder on an antique fa-
brick,

brick; and when novelty of thought is not to be obtained, the novelty of language to which we are unaccustomed, is frequently accepted as a substitute. Most poets therefore, at least such as have aspired to the sublime, have thrown their dialect at least a century behind the common prose, and colloquial phraseology of their time; nor can we entertain a doubt, but that even Shakespear and Milton have derived advantages from the antique structure of some of their most admired passages. The facility of composition is also greatly increased where full latitude is permitted in the use of an obsolete dialect; since an author is indulged in the occasional use of both the old and the modern phraseology, and if the one does not supply him with the word for which he has immediate occasion, the other in all probability will not disappoint him.

That

That the subjects of Rowley's poems are in general interesting and well chosen, cannot, I think, be doubted by the judicious reader, but still it must be confessed, that the detail is occasionally heavy, flat, and insipid. The imagery and metaphors are frequently very common-place, and it is possible to labour through several stanzas without finding any striking beauty, when the attention of the reader is kept alive by the subject alone. Many defects of style, and many passages of rant and bombast are concealed or excused by the appearance of antiquity; and where the harmony of the verse (which indeed is not often the case) is, perhaps, radically deficient, we are inclined to attribute it to a different mode of accenting, or to our ignorance of the ancient pronunciation.

The piece of most conspicuous merit in the collection, is Ella, a Tragical Interlude, which is a most complete and

well-

well-written tragedy. The plot is both
intereſting and full of variety, though the
dialogue is in ſome places tedious. The
character of Celmonde reminds us of
Glenalvon in Douglas, but it is better
drawn: His ſoliloquy is beautiful and
characteriſtic *. The firſt chorus, or
ſ Mynſtrelles Songe" in this piece, is a
perfect

* CELMONDE.

Hope, hallie ſuſter, ſweepeynge thro' the ſkie,
    In crowne of goulde, and robe of lillie whyte,
Whyche farre abrode ynne gentle ayre doe flie;
    Meetynge from diſtaunce the enjoyous ſyghte,
    Albeytte eſte thou takeſt thie hie flyghte
Hecket [1] ynne a myſte, and wyth thyne eyne yblente,
    Nowe commeſt thou to mee wythe ſtarrie lyghte;
    Ontoe thie veſte the rodde ſonne ys adente [2];
    The Sommer tyde, the month of Maie appere,
Depyćte wythe ſkylledd honde upponn thie wyde aumere.

    I from a nete of hopelen am adawed,
    Awhaped [3] atte the fetyveneſs of daie;
Ælla, bie nete moe thann hys myndbruche awed,
    Is gone, and I moſte followe, toe the fraie.
    Celmonde canne ne'er from anie byker ſtaie.
    Dothe warre begynne? there's Clemonde yn the place.
Botte

[1] Wrapped cloſely, covered.   [2] faſtened.   [3] aſtoniſh'd.

perfect paftoral. It abounds in natural
and tender fentiments, and appofite imagery, and the fertility of the author's genius

Botte whanne the warre ys donne, I'll hafte awaie.
The refte from nethe tymes mafque muft fhew yttes face.
I fee onnombered joies aronde mee ryfe ;
Blake [1] ftondethe future doome, and joie dothe mee alyfe.

O honnoure, honnoure, whatt ys bie thee hanne ?
Hailie the robber and the bordelyer,
Who kens ne thee, or ys to thee beftanne,
And nothynge does thie myckle gaftnefs fere.
Faygne woulde I from mie bofomme alle thee tare.
Thou there dyfperpelleft [2] thie levynne-bronde ;
Whyleft mie foulgh's forwyned, thou art the gare ;
Sleene ys mie comforte bie thie ferie honde ;
As fomme talle hylle, whann wynds doe fhake the ground,
Itte kerveth all abroade, bie brafteynge hyltren wounde.

Honnoure, whatt bee ytte ? tys a fhadowes fhade,
A thynge of wychencref, an idle dreme ;
On of the fonnis whych the clerche have made
Menne wydhoute fprytes, and wommen for to fleme ;
Knyghtes, who efte kenne the loude dynne of the beme,
Schulde be forgarde to fyke enfeeblynge waies,
Make everych acte, alyche theyr foules, be breme,
And for theyre chyvalrie alleyne have prayfe.
O thou, whatteer thie name,
Or Zabalus or Queed,
Comme, fteel mie fable fpryte,
For fremde [3] and dolefulle dede.

<hr>

[1] Naked,　　[2] Scattereft,　　[3] Stranger

nius is displayed in this little ballad; since short as it is, it contains a complete plot or fable *.

There

MANNE.

Tourne thee to thie Shepsterr ¹ swayne;
Bryghte sonne has ne droncke the dewe
From the floures of yellowe hue;
Tourne thee, Alyce, backe agayne.

WOMANNE.

No, bestoikerre ², I wylle go,
Softlie tryppynge o'ere the mees 3,
Lyche the sylver-footed doe,
Seekynge shelterr yn grene trees.

MANNE.

See the mofs-growne daisey'd banke,
Pereynge ynne the streme belowe;
Here we'lle sytte, yn dewie danke;
Tourne thee, Alyce, do notte goe.

WOMANNE.

I've hearde erste mie grandame saie,
Yonge damoyselles schulde ne bee,
Inne the swotie moonthe of Maie,
Wythe yonge menne bie the grene wode tree.

MANNE.

Sytte thee, Alyce, sytte and harke,
Howe the ouzle 4 chauntes hys noate,
The chelandree 5, greie morn larke,
Chauntynge from theyre lyttel throate;

WO-

---

1 Shepherd.   2 deceiver.   3 meadows.   4 The black-bird.
5 Goldfinch.

There are extant two parts, or rather two
different copies of the Battle of Haftings.
                                    Thefe

WOMANNE.

I heare them from eche grene wode tree,
Chauntynge owte fo blatauntlie [1],
Tellynge lecturnyes [2] to mee,
Myfcheefe ys whanne you are nygh.

MANNE.

See alonge the mees fo grene
Pied daifies, kynge-cöppes fwote;
Alle wee fee, bie non bee feene,
Nete botté fhepe fettes here a fote.

WOMANNE.

Shepfter fwayne, you tare mie gratche [3].
Oute uponne ye! lette me goe.
Leave mee fwythe, or I'lle alatche.
Robynne, thys youre dame fhall knowe.

MANNE.

See! the crokynge brionie
Rounde the popler twyfte hys fpraie;
Rounde the oake the greene ivie
Florryfchethe and lyveth aie.

Lette us feate us bie thys tree,
Laughe, and fynge to lovynge ayres;
Comme, and doe notte coyen bee;
Nature made all thynges bie payres.

                                    Droorled

1 Loudly.   2 lectures.   3 apparel.

These appear to have been higher in the
estimation of Chatterton, as well as of
Dr. Milles, than most of the other productions

Drooried cattes wylle after kynde;
Gentle doves wylle kyfs and coe:
WOMANNE.
Botte manne, hee moste bee ywrynde,
Tylle fyr preeste make on of two.

Tempe mee ne to the foule thynge;
I wylle no mannes lemanne be;
Tyll fyr preeste hys fonge doethe fynge,
Thou fhalt neere fynde aught of mee.
MANNE.
Bie oure ladie her yborne,
To-morrowe, foone as ytte ys daie,
I'lle make thee wyfe, ne bee forfworne,
So tyde me lyfe or dethe for aie.
WOMANNE.
Whatt dothe lette, botte thatte nowe
Wee attenes [1], thos honde yn honde,
Unto diviniftre [2] goe,
And bee lyncked yn wedlocke bonde ?
MANNE.
I agree, and thus I plyghte
Honde, and harte, and all that's myne;
Good fyr Rogerr, do us ryghte,
Make us one, at Cothbertes fhryne.
BOTHE.

[1] At once. [2] a divine.

ductions of Rowley. When Chatterton brought the firſt part to Mr. Barret, being greatly preſſed to produce the poem in the original hand-writing, he at laſt ſaid, that he had written this poem himſelf for a friend; but that he had another, the copy of an original by Rowley: and being then deſired to produce that poem, he brought, after ſome time, to Mr. Barrett, the poem which is marked in Mr. Tyrwhit's and Dr. Milles's editions, as No. 2 *.

The firſt of theſe poems I cannot help claſſing among the moſt inferior of Rowley's. The mere detail of violence and carnage, with nothing to intereſt curioſity, or engage the more tender paſſions, can

BOTHE.

We wylle ynn a bordelle [1] lyve,
Hailie, thoughe of no eſtate;
Everyche clocke moe love ſhall gyve;
Wee ynn godeneſſe wylle bee greate.

1 A cottage.

* Introd. Account prefixed to Rowley's poems, p. 23.

can be pleafing to few readers. There is
not a fingle episode to enliven the tedious
narrative, and but few of the beauties of
poetry to relieve the mind from the difgufting fubject.

The fecond part is far fuperior. There
is more of poetical defcription in it, more
of nature, more of character. The imagery is more animated, the incidents
more varied. The character of Tancar-
ville is well drawn, and the fpirit of candour and humanity which pervades it, is
perhaps unparalleled in any writer before
the age of Shakefpear. The whole epi-
fode of Gyrtha is well conducted, and the
altercation between him and his brother
Harold, is interefting. But the defcription of morning *, and that of Salifbury
plain

* And now the greie-eyd morne with vi'lets dreft,
Shakyng the dewdrops on the flourie meedes;
Fled with her rofie radiance to the Weft:
Forth from the Eafterne gatte the fyerie fteedes

M

plain *, would be alone fufficient to ref-
cue the whole poem from oblivion, and
to entitle it to a place upon a claffic fhelf.

　　　　　　　　　　　　　　　　The

Of the bright funne awaytynge fpirits leedes :
The funne, in fierie pompe enthrond on hie,
Swyfter than thoughte alonge hys jernie gledes,
And fcatters nyghtes remaynes from oute the fkie :
He fawe the armies make for bloudie fraie,
And ftopt his driving fteeds, and hid his lyghtfome raye.

 * Where fruytlefs heathes and meadows cladde in greie,
Save where derne hawthornes reare theyr humble heade;
The hungrie traveller upon his waie
Sees a huge defarte alle arounde hym fpredde,
The diftaunte citie fcantlie to be fpedde,
The curlynge force of fmoke he fees in vayne,
Tis too far diftaunte, and hys onlie bedde
Iwimpled in hys cloke ys on the playne,
Whylfte rattlynge thonder forrey oer his hedde,
And raines come down to wette hys harde uncouthlie bedde.

A wondrous pyle of rugged mountaynes ftandes,
Placd on eche other in a dreare arraie,
It ne could be the worke of human handes,
It ne was reared up bie menne of claie.
Here did the Brutons adoration paye
To the falfe god whom they did Tauran name,
Dightynge hys altarre with greete fyres in Maie,
Roaftynge their vyctualle round aboute the flame,
'Twas here that Hengyft did the Brytons flee,
As they were mette in council for to bee.

The utmoft efforts of the author, however, cannot always impart intereft or variety to the dull catalogue of names, which have ceafed to be remembered, and the unvaried recital, of wounds and deaths. But Homer himfelf nods when engaged upon a topic fo unfavourable to genius.

The Briftowe Tragedy, or the Deathe of Syr Charles Bawdin, has little but its pathetic fimplicity to recommend it. There is nothing ingenious in the plot, or ftriking in the execution; and it only ranks upon a par with a number of tragic ballads, both ancient and modern, in the fame ftyle.

The eclogues are to be accounted fome of the moft perfect fpecimens among the poems of Rowley. Indeed, I am not acquainted with any paftorals fuperior to them, either ancient or modern. The firft of them bears a remote refemblance to the firft eclogue of Virgil;

M 2

and

and contains a beautiful and pathetic pic-
ture of the ſtate of England, during the
civil wars between the houſes of York
and Lancaſter. The thoughts and images are all truly paſtoral; and it is impoſſible to read it, without experiencing
thoſe lively, yet melancholy feelings,
which a true delineation of nature alone
can inſpire. I cannot help feeling an
irreſiſtable inclination to preſent the reader with two ſtanzas, which have ever
appeared to me particularly beautiful.

RAUFE.

Saie to mee nete; I kenne thie woe in myne;
O! I've a tale that Sabalus [1] mote [2] telle.
Swote [3] flouretts, mantled meedows, foreſtes dygne [4];
Gravots [5] far-kend [6] arounde the Errmiets [7] cell;
The ſwote ribible [8] dynning [9] yn the dell;
The joyous daunceynge ynn the hoaſtrie [10] courte;
Eke [11] the highe ſonge and everych joie farewell;
Farewell the verie ſhade of fayre dyſporte [12]:
Impeſtering [13] trobble onn mie heade doe comme,
Ne on kynde Seynête to warde [14] the aye [15] encreaſyngedome.

R O-

1 The Devil.   2 might.   3 ſweet.   4 good, neat, genteel;
5 groves, ſometimes uſed for a coppice.   6 far-ſeen.   7 Hermit.
8 violin.   9 ſounding.   10 inn, or public-houſe.   11 alſo.   12 pleaſure.   13 annoying.   14 to keep off.   15 ever, always.

ROBERTE.

Oh! I coulde waile mie kynge-coppe-decked mees 16,
Mie spreedynge flockes of shepe of lillie white,
Mie tendre applynges 17, and embodyde 18 trees,
Mie Parker's Grange 19, far spreedynge to the syghte,
Mie cuyen 20 kyne 21, mie bullockes stringe 22 yn fyghte.
Mie gorne 23 emblaunched 24 with the comfreie 25 plante,
Mie floure 26 Seyncte Marie shotteyng wyth the lyghte,
Mie store of all the blessynges Heaven can grant.
I amm duressed 27 unto sorrowes blowe,
Ihanten'd 28 to the peyne, will lette ne salte teare flowe.

16 Meadows. 17 grafted trees. 18 thick, stout. 19 liberty of pasture given to the Parker. 20 tender. 21 cows. 22 strong. 23 garden. 24 whitened. 25 cumfrey, a favourite dish at that time. 26 marygold. 27 hardened. 28 accustomed.

The second eclogue is an eulogium on the actions of Richard I. in the Holy-land, which will be read with additional pleasure by those who have seen the short but spirited sketch of these wars in Mr. Gibbon's last volumes. The poem is supposed to be sung by a young shepherd, whose father is absent on the Holy war: and the Epode, or burthen, is happily imagined:

" Sprytes of the blest, and every seyncte ydedde,
" Pour out your pleasaunce on my fadre's hedde."

M 3   Before

Before he has concluded his song, he is
cheered by the fight of the veſſel in
which his father returns victorious.

The third paſtoral is chiefly to be admired for its excellent morality; it is,
however, enlivened by a variety of appro-
priate imagery, and many of the orna-
ments of true poetry.

The laſt of theſe paſtorals, called Elinoure and Juga, is one of the fineſt pathetic tales I have ever read. The complaint of two young females lamenting
their lovers ſlain in the wars of York
and Lancaſter, was one of the happieſt
ſubjects that could be choſen for a tragic
paſtoral. Two ſtanzas of this poem, will,
I flatter myſelf, amply juſtify this opinion: part of the former has been ſuppoſed, by the Anti-Rowleians, to be an
imitation of a ſtanza in Mr. Gray's elegy,

"The breezy call of incenſe breathing morn, &c."

E L I N.

ELINOURE.

No moe the miskynette [1] shall wake the morne,
The minstrelle daunce, good cheere, and morryce plaie;
No moe the amblynge palfrie and the horne
Shall from the lessel [2] rouze the foxe awaie;
I'll seke the foreste alle the lyve-longe daie;
Alle nete amenge the gravde chyrche [3] glebe will goe,
And to the passante Spryghtes lecture [4] mie tale of woe.

JUGA.

Whan mokie [5] cloudis do hange upon the leme
Of leden [6] Moon; ynn sylver mantels dyghte;
The tryppeynge Faeries weve the golden dreme
Of Selynes [7], whyche flyethe wythe the nyghte;
Thenne (botte the Seynctes forbydde!) gif to a spryte
Syrr Rychardes forme ys lyped, I'll holde dystraughte
Hys bledeynge claie-colde corse, and die eche daie ynn
    thoughte.

1 A small bagpipe. 2 in a confined sense, a bush or hedge, though sometimes used as a forest. 3 church-yard. 4 relate. 5 black. 6 decreasing. 7 happiness.

The ballad of Charity is an imitation of the moft beautiful and affecting of our Saviour's parables, the good Samaritan.—The poetical defcriptions are truly picturefque. We feel the horror of the dark, cold night; we fee "the big drops fall," and the "full flocks driving o'er

the

the plain." "The welkin opens, and
the yellow light'ning flies." "The thun-
der's rattling found moves flowly on, and
fwelling, burfts into a violent crafh; fhakes
the high fpire," &c. If Chatterton
were really the author of this poem, he
probably alluded to his own deferted fituation, fince, it is faid, he gave it to the
publifher of the Town and Country Magazine, only a month before his death:

"Hafte to thie church-glebe houfe 1 afhrewed 2 manne!
"Hafte to thie kifte 3, thie only dortoufe 4 bedde.
"Cale as the claie, whiche will gre on thie hedde,
"Is charitie and love aminge 5 highe elves;
"Knights and barons live for pleafure and themfelves."

1 The grave. 2 unfortunate. 3 coffin. 4 a fleeping room. 5 among

The lefler pieces in this collection are
not without merit. There is much elegant fatire in the two epiftles to Canynge
prefixed to Ella *; and fome ftrokes of
pleafantry in the "Storie of Canynge."
As

* I have felected the firft of thefe epiftles as a fpecimen
of the fatiric powers of Rowley. 'Tys

As a complete specimen of this author's abilities in Lyric composition, it is only necessary

'Tys songe bie mynstrelles, thatte yn auntyent tym,
Whan Reasonn hylt 1 herselfe in cloudes of nyghte,
The preeste delyvered alle the lege 2 yn rhym ;
Lyche peyncted 3 tyltynge speares to please the syghte,
The whyche yn yttes selle use doe make moke 4 dere 5,
Syke dyd theire auncyante lee deftlie 6 delyghte the eare.

Perchaunce yn Vyrtues gare 7 rhym mote bee thenne,
Butte efte 8 nowe flyeth to the odher syde ;
In hallie 9 preeste apperes the ribaudes 10 penne,
Inne lithe 11 moncke apperes the barronnes pryde :
But rhym wythe somme, as nedere 12 widhout teethe,
Make pleasaunce to the sense, botte maie do lyttel scathe 13.

Syr Johne, a knyghte, who hath a barne of lore 14,
Kenns 15 Latyn att fyrst syghte from Frenche or Greke,
Pyghethe 16 hys knowlachynge ten yeres or more,
To rynge upon the Latynne worde to speke.
Whoever spekethe Englysch ys despysed,
The Englysch hym to please moste fyrste be latynized.

Vevyan, a moncke, good a requiem 18 synges ;
Can preache so wele, eche hynde 19 hys mencynge knowes ;
Albeytte these gode guyfts awaie he flynges,
Beeynge as badde yn vearse as goode yn prose.
Hee synges of seynctes who dyed for yer Godde,
Everych wynter nyghte afresche he sheddes theyr blodde.

To

1 Hid, concealed. 2 law. 3 painted. 4 much. 5 hurt, damage. 6 sweetly. 7 cause. 8 oft. 9 holy. 10 rake, lewd person. 11 humble. 12 adder. 13 hurt, damage. 14 learning. 15 knows. 16 plucks or tortures. 17 knowledge. 18 a service used over the dead. 19 peasant.

necessary to cite the incomparable ode or chorus.

To maydens, huswyfes, and unlored 20 dames,
Hee redes hys tales of merryment & woe.
Loughe 21 loudie dynneth 22 from the dolte 23 adrames 24;
He swelles on laudes of fooles, tho' kennes 25 hem foe.
Sommetyme at tragedie theie laughe and synge,
At merric yaped 26 fage 27 somme hard-drayned water brynge.

Yette Vevyan ys ne foole, beyinde 28 hys lynes.
Geofroie makes yearse, as handycrafts theyr ware;
Wordes wythoute sense fulle groffyngelye 29 he twynes,
Cotteynge hys storie off as-wythe a sheere;
Waytes monthes on nothynge, & hys storie donne,
Ne moe you from ytte kenn, than gyf 30 you neere begonne.

Enowe of odhers; of mieselfe to write,
Requyrynge whatt I doe notte nowe possess,
To you I leave the taske; I kenne your myghte
Wyll make mie faultes, mie meynte 31 of faultes, be less.
ÆLLA wythe thys I sende, and hope that you
Wylle from ytte caste awaie, whatte lynes maie be untrue.

Playes made from hallie 32 tales I holde unmeete;
Lette somme greate storie of a manne be songe;
Whanne, as a manne, we Godde and Jesus treate,
In mie pore mynde, we doe the Godhedde wronge.
Botte lette ne wordes, whyche 33 droorie mote ne heare,
Bee placed yn the same. Adieu untyll anere 34.

THOMAS ROWLEIE.

20 Unlearned. 21 laugh. 22 sounds. 23 foolish. 24 churls.
25 knows. 26 laughable. 27 tale, jest. 28 beyond. 29 foolishly.
30 if. 31 many. 32 holy. 33 strange perversion of words. *Droorie*
in its ancient signification stood for *modesty*. 34 another.

chorus in Goddwyn, a tragedy, which he has left imperfect.

CHORUS, &c.

When Freedome, dreſte yn blodde-ſteyned veſte,
  To everie knyghte her warre-ſonge ſunge,
Uponne her hedde wylde wedes were ſpredde;
  A gorie anlace bye her honge.
        She daunced onne the heathe;
        She hearde the voice of deathe;
Pale-eyned affryghte, hys harte of ſylver hue,
In vayne aſſayled 1 her boſomme to acale 2 ;
She hearde onſlemed 3 the ſhriekinge voice of woe,
And ſadneſſe ynne the owlette-ſhake the dale.
        She ſhooke the burled 4 ſpeere,
        On hie ſhe jeſte 5 her ſheelde,
        Her foemen 6 all appere,
        And flizze 7 alonge the feelde.
Power, wythe his heafod 8 ſtraught 9 ynto the ſkyes,
Hys ſpeere a ſonne-beame, and his ſheelde a ſtarre,
Alyche 10 twaie 11 brendeynge 12 gronfyres 13 rolls hys eyes,
Chaſtes 14 with hys yronne feete and ſoundes to war.
        She ſyttes upon a rocke,
        She bendes before hys ſpeere,
        She ryſes from the ſhocke,
        Wielding her owne in ayre.
Harde as the thonder dothe ſhe drive ytte on,
Wytte ſcillye 15 wympled 16 gies 17 ytte to his crowne,.

Hys

---

1 Endeavoured. 2 freeze. 3 undiſmayed. 4 armed, pointed.
5 hoiſted on high, raiſed. 6 foes, enemies. 7 fly. 8 head. 9 ſtretched.
10 like. 11 two. 12 flaming. 13 meteors. 14 beats, ſtamps.
15 cloſely. 16 mantled, covered. 17 guides.

Hys longe ſharpe ſpere, hys ſpreddynge ſheelde is gon,
He falles; and fallynge rolleth thouſandes down.
  War, goare-faced war, bie envie burld [18], ariſt [19],
Hys feerie heaulme [20] noddynge to the ayre,
Tenne bloddie arrowes ynne hys ſtreynynge fyſte.—

    [18] Armed.   [19] aroſe.   [20] helmet.

The poems of Rowley had not been long made public, before their authenticity underwent a ſevere ſcrutiny; and a number of gentlemen converſant in antiquities, declared, that they could not be the productions of the fifteenth century, and openly pronounced them the forgeries of Chatterton. Their authenticity was defended by other perſons of no inconſiderable note in the literary world. The controverſy ſoon became voluminous; and the reader will not be inclined to conſider it as unimportant, when on one ſide the names of Walpole, Tyrwhitt, Warton*,

                                  Croft,

* I have been well informed that both Mr. Warton and Mr. Tyrwhit were formerly of ſentiments directly oppoſite to thoſe which they profeſs, in their publications; if the poems therefore be forgeries of Chatterton, theſe gentlemen were at leaſt among the firſt on whom he impoſed.

Croft, and Malone, are mentioned: and on the other, thofe of Milles and Bryant; and I think I may venture to add, that of Mr. Matthias, though his candour and modefty, almoft exempt him from being confidered as a partizan.

I fhall endeavour to exhibit a fhort fketch of the arguments on both fides of the queftion, and fhall leave my readers to form their own conclufions.

The evidence on this fubject naturally divides itfelf into two branches, external and internal: of the former, there is little fatisfactory to be obtained; and it muft be confeffed, that the bulk of the external evidence is rather againft that party, which denies the authenticity of the poems. There are, however, a few facts on that fide of the queftion which are of too much confequence to be difregarded.

ARGU-

ARGUMENTS AGAINST the AUTHEN-
TICITY of ROWLEY's POEMS.

External Evidence.

I. The first serious objection which occurs against the authenticity of the poems,
is, that Chatterton never could be prevailed
upon to produce more than four of the
originals, and these extremely short, the
whole not containing more than 124
verses *. Had such a treasure of ancient
poetry fallen into the hands of a young
and ingenuous person, would he, it is said,
have cautiously produced them to the
world one by one? Would he not rather
have been proud of his good fortune?
Would not the communicativeness of youth
have induced him to blaze the discovery
abroad, and to call every lover of poetry
and antiquity, to a participation of the
pleasure?

* Tyrwhitt's Vindication, p. 133.

pleafure? Would not the hope and offers
of reward at leaft have prevented his de-
ftroying what, if preferved, would certainly
be productive of profit, but the deftruction of which could anfwer no purpofe
whatever.* ?

II. The deficiency of proof in favour
of Rowley, is ftrongly aided by the very
probable proofs in favour of Chatterton.
His abilities were in every refpect calculated for fuch a deception. He had been
in the habit of writing verfes from his
earlieft youth, and produced fome excellent poetry. He was known to have been
converfant with our old Englifh poets
and hiftorians, particularly Chaucer. His
fondnefs for heraldry, introduced many
books of antiquities to his notice; and
even

---

* An examination, &c. p. 9. Tyrwhitt's Vindication,
p. 155. See alfo fome excellent remarks to the fame purpofe, by the late Mr. Badcock, Monthly Review for May,
1782.

even his profession disposed him to these studies, and enabled him with facility to imitate ancient writings. In *the Christmas games*, which are acknowledged to be his own, there is much of that peculiar learning in British antiquities, which was necessary to lay the foundation of Rowley's poems; and in his Essay on Sculpture, there is much of the same general information with which those compositions abound *. The transport and delight,

---

* In the supplement to the works of Chatterton, (printed for Becket, 1784,) there is inserted a piece which has been already referred to, called Chatterton's will. This appears to have been written a few days before he left Bristol to go to London; when in consequence, as it should seem, of his being refused a small sum of money by a gentleman, whom he had occasionally complimented in his poems, he had taken a resolution of destroying himself the next day. What prevented him from carrying this design at that time into execution does not appear; but the whole writing on this occasion is worth attention, as it throws much light on his real character, his acquaintance with old English writers, and his capability of understanding and imitating old French and Latin inscriptions, not indeed gramatically, but sufficient to answer the purposes

light, which Chatterton always difcovered
on reading the poems to Mr. Smith; his
fifter, and his different friends, could not,
it is faid, have refulted from the mere
pleafure of a difcovery: it was the fecret, but ardent feeling of his own abilities, and the confcioufnefs that the praifes
which were beftowed upon them were all
his own, which filled him with exultation,
and

to which he often applied this knowledge. From this
writing it alfo appears that he would not allow King David
to have been a holy man, from the ftrains of piety and
devotion in his pfalms, becaufe a *great genius can effect any
thing*; that is, *affume* any *character* and *mode* of *writing* he
pleafes. This is an anfwer from Chatterton himfelf, to one
argument; and a very powerful one, in fupport of the authenticity of Rowley's poems. In that part of the will addreffed to Mr. George Catcot, Chatterton mentions Rowley's poems, but in fo guarded a manner, that it is not
eafy to draw any certain information for or againft their
authenticity; though the parties on both fides have attempted it. The addrefs to Mr. Barrett does no lefs
credit to his own feelings, than to that gentleman's treatment of him; and the apology that follows to the two Mr.
Catcotts, for fome effufions of his fatire upon them, is
the beft recompence he then had in his power to make to
thofe gentlemen, from whom he had experienced much
civility and kindnefs. O.

N

and produced those strong emotions, which even his habitual reserve on this subject was unable to conceal *.

III. The declaration of Chatterton to Mr. Barrett, concerning the first part of the Battle of Haftings, which he confessed *he had written himself*, is a presumption against the rest. He was then taken by surprize, but at other times preserved a degree of confistency in his falsehood.

IV. Mr. Ruddall, an intimate acquaintance of Chatterton, declared to Mr. Croft, that he saw him (Chatterton) disguise several pieces of parchment with the appearances of age, and that Chatterton told him, that the parchment which Mr. Ruddall had assisted him in blacking and disguising, was the very parchment he had sent to the printer's, containing

* Monthly Review for March 1782.

taining " the account of the Fryers paffing the old bridge *."

V. The

* " To GEORGE STEEVENS, Efq. Hampſtead Heath.

" DEAR SIR,

" IT gives me pleaſure that LOVE AND MADNESS, which
I put together in a few idle hours, as much for the ſake of
doing juſtice to poor Chatterton as of blunting the edge of
Hackman's ſhocking example, has ſo well anſwered the
former purpoſe.

" ————— Where'er (his bones at reſte)
" His ſpryte to haunte delyghteth beſte,"
Chatterton muſt be now not a little gratified when he looks
down upon the ſquabbles he has raiſed on earth. Every
ſyllable which I have made Hackman relate of him in LOVE
AND MADNESS is, I firmly believe, religiouſly true. I
Walmſly was my tenant for the houſe in Shoreditch, where
Chatterton lodged with him, at the time he gave me the
information contained in my book. Chatterton's letters
which I printed, and which are hardly leſs ſingular perhaps
than Rowley's poems, are confeſſedly original.

" As I cannot ſpare time from my profeſſion to enter any
further into this diſpute, and as you inform me that Mr.
Warton is going to publiſh ſomething, I write this letter,
according to your deſire, in anſwer to your's of yeſterday,
reſpecting what long ſince I ſaid to you of Mr. Ruddall;
and it is perfectly at Mr. Warton's ſervice. But I muſt
deſire he will print it exactly as I ſend it you. When I
have ſpoken for myſelf, he may draw his own arguments
from my communication.

N 2

" The

V. The Rev. Mr. Catcott, brother to the Mr. Catcott before mentioned, affirmed,

" The left hand column is an extract from Dean Milles's quarto edition of Rowley's, i. e. of Chatterton's poems, p. 436, 7. The right hand column is my account of the same business. In some material circumstances he certainly errs. It were easy to shew, the Dean has condemned Chatterton, and robbed him of Rowley's poems upon slighter evidence of less material mistakes.

" That the Dean should have received *all* his information of this business from Mr. Ruddall, is certainly impossible, because some part of his account of it is certainly untrue. The passages in the Dean's account, on which I comment, are marked, that they may be printed in Italics.

" A *singular* circumstance relating to the history of this ceremony (" of passing the " old bridge") *has been communicated to the Publick within these two last years;* and candour requires that it should not pass unnoticed here, especially as the character of the relator leaves no room for suspicion. The objectors to the authenticity of these poems may possibly triumph in the discovery of a fact, which contains, in their opinion, a decisive proof that Chatterton

The circumstance is singular, and I have always thought so; but it has never yet, I believe, been *communicated to the Publick*; though I certainly meant it should some time or other.

firmed, that having had a conversation one evening with Chatterton, he traced the very

Chatterton was the author of this paper, and (as they would infer) of all the poetry which he produced under Rowley's name; but, *when the circumstances are attentively examined*, the reader will probably find, that even this fact tends rather to establish, than to invalidate, the authenticity of the poems.

Mr. John Ruddall, a native and inhabitant of Bristol, and formerly apprentice to Mr. Francis Gresley, an apothecary in that city, was well acquainted with Chatterton, whilst he was apprentice to Mr. Lambert. During that time, Chatterton frequently called upon him at his master's house, and, *soon after he had printed this account of the Bridge* in the Bristol paper, *told Mr. Ruddall, that he was the author of it; but, it occuring to him afterwards, that he might be called upon to produce the original, he brought*

It is not clear to me, that the advocates for Chatterton have occasion to be apprehensive, *if the circumstances should be attentively examined* even according to the Dean's own shewing. But mine is somewhat different.

My

very ſubſtance of this converſation, in a piece which that indefatigable genius produced ſometime after as Rowley's.

VI. Chat—

to him one day a piece of Parchment, about the ſize of a half Sheet of Fool's - Cap paper; Mr. Ruddall does not think that any thing was written on it when produced by Chatterton, but he ſaw him write ſeveral Words, if not lines, in a Character which Mr. Ruddall did not underſtand, which he ſays was totally unlike Engliſh, and, as he apprehended, was meant by Chatterton, to imitate or repreſent the original from which this Account was printed. He cannot determine preciſely how much Chatterton wrote in this manner, but ſays, that the time he ſpent in that Viſit did not exceed three quarters of an hour; the Size of the Parchment, however, (even ſuppoſing it to have been filled with writing) will in ſome meaſure aſcertain the quantity which it contained.

My viſit to Briſtol of a few days, in order to collect information concerning Chatterton, was on the 23d of July, 1778. At that time I gave ſomething to the Mother and Siſter for their voluntary communications to me. After I publiſhed LOVE AND MADNESS, I laid a larger plan for their benefit, which I hope ſtill to ſee carried into execution; and I deſtined ſomething more to the family of him whoſe genius I ſo much reſpected, though I well knew his family deemed me their enemy for endeavouring to prove him guilty of Forgery. Prevented from going to Bath, and conſequently from giving what I had ſet apart for this purpoſe, with my own Hands, I gladly ſeized the liberty allowed me by a friend of Mr. Ruddall to beg this favour of him. On the

VI. Chatterton at firſt exhibited the Songe to Ella in his own hand-writing; and afterwards in the parchment, which he gave

the 22d of March, 1781, I wrote to Mr. Ruddall, to whom I was then a perfect ſtranger, making uſe of his Friend's name, and encloſing a Draught to him or his order for ten pounds, requeſting he would give the Money to Chatterton's Mother and Siſter. On the 30th of the ſame Month, Mr. Ruddall called upon me in Lincoln's Inn; appeared, as I imagined, to lean to the ſide of this queſtion which I have ever thought to be the right; and told me, of his own accord, what certainly agrees no more with the Dean's account, than what I have already related agrees with the Dean's ſaying that Mr. Ruddall told this, *in 1779, on the proſpect of procuring a gratuity of ten Pounds for Chatterton's Mother, from a Gentleman who came to Briſ-*

gave to Mr. Barrett as the original, there were found several variations, which it is supposed

tol in order to collect information concerning the Son's History.

He says also, that *when Chatterton had written on the Parchment, he held it over the Candle, to give it the appearance of antiquity, which changed the Colour of the Ink, and made the Parchment appear black and a little contracted: he never saw him make any similar attempt, nor was the Parchment produced afterwards by Chatterton to him; or (as far as he knows) to any other person. From a perfect knowledge of Chatterton's abilities, he thinks him to have been incapable of writing the Battle of Hastings, or any of those Poems produced by him under the name of Rowley,* nor does he remember that Chatterton ever mentioned Rowley's Poems to him, either as original, or the contrary; but sometimes (though very rarely) intimated

If my Memory not only fails me now, but failed me the same day, and has failed me ever since, Mr. Ruddall will correct me. To him I appeal, and by him I must submit to be corrected. But, on the 30th of March, 1781, he told me, AS I THINK, that *he assisted Chatterton in disguising* SEVERAL *pieces of Parchment with the appearances of Age, just before "the "Account of passing the "Bridge" appeared in Farley's Journal; that, after they had made several experiments, Chatterton said, "this will "do, now I will black* THE "*Parchment;" that, whe-. ther he told him at the time what* THE *Parchment was, he could not remember; that he believed he did not see Chatterton black* THE *Parchment, but that Chatterton told him, after

fuppofed he had admitted through forget-
fulnefs, or perhaps, as actual corrections,
considering

mated that he was poffeffed
of fome valuable literary productions. Mr. Ruddall had
promifed Chatterton not to reveal this Secret, and he fcru-
pulo'fly kept his word till the
year 1779; but, ON THE
PROSPECT OF PROCURING
A GRATUITY OF TEN
POUNDS, FOR CHATTER-
TON'S MOTHER, FROM A
GENTLEMAN WHO CAME
TO BRISTOL IN ORDER TO
COLLECT INFORMATION
CONCERNING HER SON'S
HISTORY, he thought fo
material a benefit to the Family would fully juftify him
for divulging a fecret by
which no perfon now living
could be a fufferer."

after " the Account of paf-
" fing the Bridge" had appeared in the News-paper,
that THE Parchment which
he had blacked and difguifed,
after their experiments, was
what he had fent to the Printer
containing the ACCOUNT."

" As this appeared to me the moft decifive evidence, I
afked Mr. Ruddall's leave to make ufe of his name about
it, which he granted me; and I made a Memorandum of
it, the fame day, at the diftance of a few hours. But it is
ftill poffible my Memory might deceive me. In matters
more ferious than the authenticity of Poems, which are
certainly

considering that the parchment was the copy which probably would be resorted to as a standard *.

VII. The

certainly exquisite, whoever wrote them, it is not my way, I hope, to be more positive than I ought.

"Mr. Ruddall will excuse me if I say, that I cannot possibly allow him, or any one, to determine the authenticity of the Poems, by telling the Dean, or the world, that, "*from a perfect knowledge of Chatterton's abilities,* HE "thinks him to have been incapable of writing the Battle of "Haftings, or any of thofe Poems produced by him under "the name of Rowley."

"It appears to me that I cannot poffibly, all this time, have been noticing what does not relate to me, becaufe Chatterton's Sifter, when fhe thanks me in a Letter dated April the 20th, 1781, for what I fent her and her Mother, through Mr. Ruddall, says, that "the only benefits they "have reaped from *the labours of her dear Brother,*" are what they have received from me.

"Convey this to Mr. Warton, if you choofe it, with many thanks for the pleafure I have received from his Hiftory of English Poetry; and believe me to be,

"Dear Sir,

"Your obliged friend,

Lincolns-Inn,   "HERBERT CROFT, jun."
Feb. 5, 1782.

* Curfory Obfervations on Rowley's poems, p. 44.

VII. The hand-writing of the frag-ment containing the ftorie of W. Can-ynge, is quite different from the hand-writing of that which contains " the accounte of W. Canyinge's feaft;" and neither of them is written in the ufual record hand of the age to which they are attributed. Indeed, in the " accounte of W. Canynge's Feafte," the Arabian numerals, (63) are faid to be perfectly modern, totally different from the figures ufed in the fifteenth century, and exactly fuch as Chatterton himfelf was accuftom-ed to make *.

VIII. The very exiftence of any fuch perfon as ROWLEY is queftioned, and up-on apparently good ground. He is not fo much as noticed by William of Worceftre, who lived nearly about the fuppofed time of Rowley, was himfelf of Briftol, and makes

frequent

* See Milles's Rowley, p. 429. Tyrwhitt's Vindication, p. 135. Monthly Review, by Badcock, for March 1782.

frequent mention of Canynge. " Bale,
who lived two hundred years nearer to
Rowley than we, and who, by unwearried
induftry, dug a thoufand bad authors out
of obfcurity," has never taken the leaft
notice of fuch a perfon*; nor yet Leland,
Pitts, or Tanner, nor indeed any other literary biographer. That no copies of any
of his works fhould exift, but thofe depofited in Redcliffe church, is alfo an un-
accountable circumftance not eafy to be
furmounted †.

IX. Objections are even made to the
manner in which the poems are faid to
have been preferved. That title deeds
relating to the church or even hiftorical
records might be lodged in the muniment room of Redcliffe church, is allowed to be fufficiently probable; but that
poems fhould have been configned to a
cheft

* Walpole's two letters; p. 31.
† Tyrwhitt's Vindication, p. 119, 121.

cheſt with ſix keys, kept in a private room in a church with title deeds and con‐veyances, and that theſe keys ſhould be in‐truſted, not to the heads of a college, or any literary ſociety, but to aldermen and church-wardens, is a ſuppoſition replete with abſurdity; and the improbability is increaſed, when we conſider that theſe very papers paſſed through the hands of perſons of ſome literature, of Chatterton's father in particular, who had a taſte for poetry, and yet without the leaſt diſcovery of their intrinſic value *.

Internal Evidence.

I. In point of STYLE, COMPOSITION, and SENTIMENT, it is urged by Mr. Warton, and thoſe who adopt the ſame ſide of the controverſy, that the poems of Rowley are infinitely ſuperior to every other production of the century, which is

said

---

* See Monthly Review for March 1782.

said to have produced them. Our ancient poets are minute and particular,
they do not deal in abstraction and general
exhibition, but dwell on realities; but
the writer of these poems adopts ideal
terms and artificial modes of explaining
a fact, and employs too frequently the aid
of metaphor, and personification*. Our
ancient bards abound in unnatural concep-
tions, strange imaginations, and even the
most ridiculous inconsistencies; but Rowley's poems present us with no incongru-
ous combinations, no mixture of manners, institutions, usages and characters:
they contain no violent or gross impro-
prieties †. One of the striking characteristics of old English poetry, is a continued tenor of disparity. In Gower,
Chaucer, and Lydgate, elegant descrip-
tions, ornamental images, &c. bear no
proportion

---

* Matthias's Essay on Evid, p. 64.
† Warton's Inquiry, p. 21.

proportion to pages of languor, medio-
crity, profaic and uninterefting details;
but the poems in queftion are uniformly
fupported, and are throughout poetical and
animated *. Poetry, like other fciences
(fay thefe critics) has its gradual acceffions
and advancements; and the poems in queftion poffefs all that elegance, firmnefs of
contexture, ftrength and brilliancy, which
did not appear in our poetry before the
middle of the prefent century.

II. There appears in thefe poems none
of that LEARNING, which peculiarly
marks all the compofitions of the fifteenth century. Our old poets are perpetually confounding Gothic and claffical allufions; Ovid and St. Auftin are
fometimes cited in the fame line. A ftu-
dious ecclefiaftic of that period would
give us a variety of ufelefs authorities
from

* Ibid. p. 20; Monthly Review, May 1782.

from Ariftotle, from Boethius, and from
the Fathers.: and the whole would be in-
terfperfed with allufions to another kind
of reading, viz. the old romances; the
round table, with Sir Launcelott, and
Sir Triftram, and Charlemagne, would
have been conftantly cited *. Poems from
fuch an author, would alfo have occafionally exhibited prolix devotional epifodes,
mingled with texts of Scripture, and ad-
dreffes to the Saints and bleffed Virgin;
inftead of apoftrophes to fuch allegori-
cal divinities as Truth and Content, and
others of Pagan original †.

As to the hiftorical allufions which are
really found in thefe poems, it is afferted,
that they are only fuch as might be fup-
plied by books which are eafily obtained,
fuch as Hollingfhead and Fox, Fuller's
church hiftory, Geofry of Mohmouth, and
others

* Warton's Inquiry, 21, 97, 99.
† Ibid 98.

others of a similar nature * ; and that
general reading has been mistaken for profound erudition † .

III. Some ANACHRONISMS have also
been pointed out in the manuscripts of
Rowley. Thus the art of *knitting stock-
ings* is alluded to in the Tragedy of
Ella ‡ ; whereas it is a well established
fact,

---

* Matthias's Essay, p. 69. An Examination of Rowley's
Poems, p. 24.

† Warton's Inquiry.

‡ As Elynour bie the green lesselle was syttynge,
    As from the fones hete she harried,
  She sayde, as herr whytte hondes whyte hosen was knyt
        tynge,
    Whatte pleasure ytt ys to be married!

  Mie husbande, Lorde Thomas, a forrester boulde,
    As ever clove pynne, or the baskette,
  Does no cherysauncys from Elynour houlde,
    I have ytte as soone as I aske ytte.

  Whann I lyved wyth mie fadre yn merrie Clowd-dell,
    Tho' twas at my liefe to mynde spynnynge,
  I stylle wanted somethynge, botte whatte ne coulde telle,
    Mie lorde fadres barbde haulle han ne wynnynge.

O Eche

fact, that the art was utterly unknown in the reign of Edward IV. Bristol is called a city, though it was not such till long after the death of that monarch. Canynge is said to have possessed a *cabinet* of coins, *drawings*, &c. though these words were not then in use; and *manuscripts* are spoken of as rarities, at a time when there were scarcely any other books: when, in truth, a printed book must have been a much greater curiosity *.

IV. The

Eche monynge I ryse, doe I sette mie maydennes,
  Somme to spynn, somme to curdell, somme bleachynge,
Gyff any new entered doe aske for mie aidens,
  Tham swythynne you fynde mee a teachynge.

Lorde Walterre, mie fadre, he loved me welle,
  And nothynge unto mee was nedeynge,
Botte schulde I agen goe to merrie Cloud-dell,
  In sothen twoulde bee wythoute redeynge.

Shee sayde, and lorde Thomas came over the lea,
  As hee the fatte derkynnes wae chacynge,
Shee putte uppe her knyttynge, and to hym wente shee;
  So wee leave hem bothe kyndelie embracynge.

* Cursory Observations on Rowley's poems, p. 22—25.

IV. The METRE of the old Englifh
poetry, is faid to be totally different from
that of Rowley. The ftanza in which
the majority of thefe poems are written,
confifts of ten lines, the two firft qua-
trains of which rhyme alternately, and it
clofes with an alexandrine; no example
of which occurs in Chaucer, Lydgate or
Gower. Spencer extended the old octavo
ftanza to nine lines, clofing with an alexandrine, to which Prior added a tenth *.
Above all, the extraordinary inftance of an
Englifh Pindaric in the fifteenth century,
is ridiculed by Mr. Warton, which novelty (he fays) " was referved for the
capricious ambition of Cowley's mufe."
That Rowley fhould ever have feen the
original model of this irregular ftyle of
compofition, is utterly improbable, fince

O 2   Pindar

* Matthias's Effay, p. 66.

Pindar was one of the laſt claſſics that
emerged at the reſtoration of literature *.

   To this head may be refered the extraordinary *ſmoothneſs of the verſe,* which
is utterly unparalleled in any poet for
more than a century after the ſuppoſed
age of Rowley †; the accent or cadence,
which is always modern; and the perfection and harmony of the rhyme ‡.

   V. While the compoſition, metre, &c.
are wholly modern, the LANGUAGE is
aſſerted to be too ancient for the date of
the poems. It is not the language of
any particular period, but of two entire
centuries §. The diction and verſification
are at perpetual variance ‖. The author
appears to have borrowed all his ancient
language, not from the uſage of common
life,

---

* Warton's Inquiry, p. 33, 39.
† Curſory Obſervations, p. 5.
‡ Matthias's Eſſay, p. 67.
§ Curſory Obſervations, p. 32.
‖ Warton's Inquiry, p. 42.

life, but from Speght, Skinner, and other lexicographers, and to have copied their miftakes *. He has even introduced words which never made a part of the Englifh language, and which are evidently the coinage of fancy, analogy, or miftake †.

VI. Notwithftanding this affectation of ancient language, it is added, that the tinfel of MODERN PHRASEOLOGY may in too many inftances be detected. Thus fuch phrafes as " *Puerilitie*; *before* his *optics*; *blamelefs* tongue; the aucthoure of the *piece*; veffel wreckt upon the *tragic* fand; the *proto-fleyne* man," &c. could not be the language of the fifteenth century. We find alfo a number of modern formularies and combinations, e. g. " Syfters in forrow; poygnant arrowes *typp'd* with deftinie; Oh, Goddes !

O 3 Now

---

* Matthias's Effay, p. 68. Tyrwhitt's Appendix to Rowley's Poems, and Vindication paffim.

† Ibid.

"Now by the Goddes; Ah, what avaulde;
Awaie, awaie! (which is the cant of modern tragedy) Oh, thou, whate'er thie
name;" with a number of compound epi-
thets *, and other almoft certain marks
of modern compofition †.

VIII. To thefe may be added fome paffages which appear to be imitations of
modern poets. Many of thofe, which
have been cited to convict Chatterton of
plagiarifm, are, it muft be confeffed, fuch
obvious thoughts, that they might be
adopted by a perfon who had never feen
the modern publications in which they
appear; but fuch coincidences as the following are palpable:

" O! for a mufe of fire!"	Shakef. Hen. V.
" O forre a fpryte al feere!"	Ella, l. 729.
" His beard all white as fnow.	
". All flaxen was his pole."	Hamlet.

" Black'

* Warton's Inquiry, p. 23, 24.
† Curfory Obfervations, p. 12, 13.

"Black his cryne as the winter nyghte,
"White his rode, as the fommer fnowe." Ella, l. 851,

"No, no, he is dead,
"Gone to his death bed."   Hamlet.

"Mie love is dedde,
"Gone to his deathe-bedde."   Ella, I. 855.

"Unhoufell'd, unanointed, *unaknell'd*,"
            Hamlet in Pope's edit.
"Unburied, undelievre, unefpryte." Goddwyn, l. 27.
"Their fouls from corpfes *unaknell'd* depart."
        Bat. of Haft. part 1, l. 288.

"The grey-goofe wing that was thereon,
"In his hearts-blood was wet."   Chevy-Chace.

"The *grey-goofe* pynion, that *thereon* was fett,
"Eftfoons wyth fmokyng *crimfon bloud was wett.*"
        Bat. of Haft. part 1, l. 200.

With fuch a force and vehement might
   He did his body gore,
The fpear went thro' the other fide
   A large *cloth-yard* and *more.*   Chevy-Chace.

With thilk a force it *did his body gore,*
That in his tender guts it entered,
In veritie, a full *cloth-yard or more.*   Bat. of Haft *.

"Clos'd his eyes in endlefs night."   Gray's bard.
"He clos'd his eyne in everlaftynge nyghte."
      Bat. of Haft. part 2. l. 278 †.
       O 4   The

* See Monthly Review.
† See a letter prefixed to Chatterton's Mifcellanies, p. 24.

The advocates of Rowley, are, however, not deftitute of arguments in their fupport; I fhall therefore divide the evidence in the fame manner as in ftating the former, and endeavour to exhibit as fair a fummary as poffible.

ARGUMENTS TO PROVE THAT THE POEMS ATTRIBUTED TO ROWLEY, WERE REALLY WRITTEN BY HIM AND OTHERS IN THE 15th CENTURY.

External Evidence.

I. The firft grand argument which the advocates on this fide advance, is the conftant and uniform affertion (except in a fingle inftance) of Chatterton himfelf, who is reprefented by his fifter, and all his intimates, as a lover of truth from the earlieft dawn of reafon. He was alfo moft infatiable of fame, and abounded in vanity. He felt himfelf neglected, and many paf-

fages

fages of his writings are full of invective
on this fubject. Is it probable, that fuch
a perfon fhould barter the fair character of
truth, which he loved, for the fake of
perfifting in falfehood, which he deteft-
ed? Is it probable, that a perfon of his
confummate vanity, fhould uniformly give
the honour of all his more excellent compofitions to another, and only infcribe his
name to thofe which were evidently inferior? But even though a man might
be thus carelefs of his reputation during
his life time, under the conviction that
he might affume the honour whenever he
pleafed, would this carelefsnefs continue
even at the hour of death? Would he at
a moment, when he actually meditated
his own deftruction; in a paper which he
infcribes—" All this wrote between 11
and 2 o'clock Saturday (Evening), in the
utmoft diftrefs of mind,"—ftill repeat
with the utmoft folemnity the fame falfe
                                        affertion

aſſertion that he had affirmed during the former part of his life? there was at leaſt *no occaſion* to introduce the ſubject at that time, and he might have been ſilent, if he did not chuſe to cloſe his exiſtence with a direct falſehood *. If we conſider the joy which he manifeſted on the diſcovery of the parchments, the avidity with which he read them, he muſt be the moſt complete of diſſemblers, if really they contained no ſuch treaſure as he pretended. To another very extraordinary circumſtance Mr. Catcott has pledged himſelf, which is, that on his firſt acquaintance with Chatterton, the latter mentioned by *name* almoſt all the poems which have ſince appeared in print, and that at a time, when, if he were the author, one-tenth of them could not be written †.

II. Next

---

* See Chatterton's will, Appendix to Miſcellanies. See alſo the learned Mr. Bryant's Obſervations, p. 499, 547.
† Ibid. 548.

II. Next to the affeverations of Chatterton himfelf, we are bound to pay at leaft fome attention to thofe of all his friends. His mother accurately remembers the whole tranfaction concerning the parchments, as I have already ftated it. His fifter alfo recollects to have feen the original parchment of the poem on our Lady's Church, and, fhe thinks, of the Battle of Haftings: fhe remembers to have heard her brother mention frequently the names of Turgot, and of John Stowe, befides that of Rowley. * Mr. Smith, who was one of the moft intimate friends of Chatterton, remembers to have feen manufcripts upon vellum, to the number of a dozen in his poffeffion, many of them ornamented with the heads of kings or of popes, and fome of them as broad as the bottom of a large fized chair †. He

ufed

---

* Milles's Preliminary Differtation, p. 8.
† Bryant's Obfervations, p. 528.

ufed frequently to read to Mr. Smith,
fometimes parts, and fometimes whole
treatifes from thefe old manufcripts; and
Mr. Smith has very often been prefent
while he tranfcribed them at Mr. Lambert's *. Mr. Capel, a jeweller, at Briftol,
affured Mr. Bryant, that he had frequently called upon Chatterton, while at Mr.
Lambert's, and had at times found him
tranfcribing ancient manufcripts anfwer-
ing to the former defcription †. Mr.
Thiftlethwaite, in the curious letter already quoted, relates, that during the
year 1768, " at divers vifits, he found
Chatterton employed in copying Rowley
from what he ftill confiders as undoubted
originals ‡." Mr. Carey alfo, another
intimate acquaintance, frequently heard
Chatterton mention thefe manufcripts
foon after he left Colfton's fchool. Every
one

* Bryant's Obfervations.
† Ibid, p. 523.
‡ Milles's Rowley, p. 457.

one of thefe gentlemen; as well as Mr.
Clayfield and Mr. Ruddall, declare un-
equivocally, from an intimate knowledge
of Chatterton's learning and abililies, that
they believe him incapable of producing
the poems of Rowley.

III. That a number of manufcripts
were found in Redcliffe church, cannot
poffibly be doubted after the variety of
evidence which has been adduced to that
purpofe. Perrot, the old Sexton, who
fucceeded Chatterton's great uncle, took
Mr. Shiercliffe, a miniature painter, of
Briftol, as early as the year 1749, through
Redcliffe church; he fhewed him in the
North porch a number of parchments,
fome loofe and fome tied up, and intimated, " that there were things there,
which would one day be better known;
and that in proper hands, they might
prove a treafure *." Many of the manuscripts

* Bryant's Obfervations, p. 513.

nufcripts in Mr. Barrett's hands bear all the marks of age, and are "figned by Rowley himfelf. The characters in each inftance appear to be fimilar; and tho hand-writing the fame in all *."

IV. The fhort time which Chatterton had to produce all thefe poems, is an extraordinary circumftance. It has been already ftated, that he continued at Coulfton's fchool from the age of eight till that of fourteen and feven months : that he continued each day in fchool from feven or eight o'clock till twelve in the morning, and from one till four or five in the evening, and went to bed at eight. There is alfo reafon to believe, that he

did

---

* Bryant's Obfervations p. 548. Mr. Barrett, and he only, has it in his power finally to determine the controverfy concerning Rowley's poems. Let him produce all the manufcripts which he obtained from Chatterton, and let them be put into the hands of fome perfons converfant in old writings, who may poffibly be able to decide concerning the probable date of the hand-writing. O.

did not difcover or begin to copy thefe
poems, or even to apply himfelf to antiquities, before the age of fifteen. In about
the fpace therefore of two years and a
half, he made himfelf mafter of the ancient language of this country; he produced more than two volumes of poetry,
which are publifhed, and about as many
compofitions, in profe and verfe; as would
nearly fill two volumes more. During
this time he muft have read a confiderable
variety of books. He was ftudying me-
dicine, heraldry, and other fciences; he
was practicing drawing; he copied a large
book of precedents; and Mr. Lambert's
bufinefs, though not extenfive, muft have
occupied at leaft fome part of his attention. Which, therefore, is the eafier
fuppofition, fay the advocates for Rowley, that this almoft miracle of induftry
or ability was performed by a boy; or

that

that Chatterton really copied the poems from ancient documents * ?

V. Chat-

* Of thefe old writings, which he is fuppofed to have tranfcribed from obfcure and almoft illegible manufcripts, (exclufive of his miscellaneous and political writings,) the poetical alone fills 288 octavo pages in Mr. Tywrhitt's edition; and perhaps there are others, with a quantity of profe writings which might fill another fuch volume. See Milles's edition, p. 438.

Thefe muft have been tranfcribed by him, either in Mr. Lambert's office, or during the few hours he fpent at home with his mother in an evening. Neither Mr. Lambert nor his mother or fifter, take upon them to fay, that they ever faw him this way employed. When not engaged in the immediate bufinefs of his profeffion, he was employed by his mafter to copy forms and precedents, as well to improve him in the law as to keep him employed. Of thefe legal forms and precedents, Mr. Lambert has in his poffeffion a folio book containing 334 pages, clofely written by Chatterton; alfo 36 pages in another. In the noting book, 36 notarial acts; and in the letter book, 38 letters copied. Add to all this his own acknowledged compofitions, filling 240 pages in the printed copy, and perhaps as many more in manufcript not yet publifhed.

The greateft part of thefe compofitions, both under Rowley's name and his own, was written before he went to London, in April 1770, he being then aged 17 years and five months; and of the former, Rowley's pieces, they were almoft all exhibited a twelve month earlier, before April 1769.

Now

V. Chatterton is faid further to have difcovered great marks of ignorance on the
manufcripts coming firft into his poffeffion.
He read the name *Roulie* inftead of Rowley,
till he was fet right by Mr. Barrett *.
In the acknowledged writings of Chatterton, there are alfo palpable miftakes, and
marks of ignorance in hiftory, geography,
&c.; whereas no fuch appear in the poems
of Rowley †.   But what is of ftill greater
confequence, Mr. Bryant has laboured to
prove, that in almoft innumerable inftances, Chatterton did not underftand the
language of Rowley, but that he has ac-

P   tually

Now the time taken up in preparing the parchment and
imitating the old writing, muft probably have been greater
than the time fpent in compofing them. If he was in poffeffion of the originals, furely he would not have beftowed
all this time and pains in tranfcribing from originals, which
he might have parted with to greater advantage; and if
he did tranfcribe them, why deftroy the greateft part of
them, and exhibit only fcraps and detached lines, for fuch
only appear now to exift ? O.

* Remarks on Warton, p. 9.

† Bryant's Obfervations, p. 477.

tually misinterpreted, and sometimes mis-
transcribed him. Thus in "the English metamorphosis," ver. 14.

"Their myghte is *knopped* ynne the froste of fere."

Chatterton having recourse to Chaucer
and Skinner, has interpreted to *knop*, to *tie*,
or *fasten* ; whereas it really means, and the
context requires that it should mean, to
nip. Thus in the Second Battle of Hastings, 548, describing a sacrifice:

. "Roastynge their *vyctualle* round about the flame;".

which Mr. Tyrwhitt himself has allowed
ought to be *vyctimes*, and has accordingly
cancelled the other word. Thus in Ella,
v. 678, we find:

" Theyre throngynge corses shall *onlyghte* the starres."

The word *onlyghte*, Chatterton has here
strangely applied as meaning to *darken* the
stars, whereas Mr. Byrant, by recurring to
the Saxon, very reasonably supposes *on-
lych*

lych to have been the proper word, and the line will then mean to *be like*, or to equal the ftars in number. The word *cheri-faunei*, which Chatterton has inferted in the "Introductionne to Ella," never did really exift, and Mr. Bryant fhews that the original word was certainly *cherifaunce*: and in the Second Eclogue, Chatterton has explained the word *amenufed*, by *leff-ened*, or *diminifhed*; whereas the fame able critic fhews, that it never had any fuch meaning, but that it really fignifies *ac-curfed* or *abominable*. Thefe and other fimilar miftakes (of which Mr. Bryant fpecifies a great number) he afferts, could never have happened, had Chatterton been any more than the mere tranfcriber of thefe extraordinary poems *.

VI. With refpect to the objection, that Rowley is not mentioned by other wri-ters, it is anfwered, that there exifted fo

P 2 little

* See Mr. Bryant's Obfervations; paffim.

little communication among mankind at
that time, that Leland, who is a very
curious writer, never makes the fmalleft
mention of Canynge, Lydgate, or Oc-
cleve. That William of Worceftre, does
not mention Rowley, becaufe, unlefs hiftory demands it, writers do not commonly
commemorate perfons before their death,
and Rowley was apparently alive when
William of Worceftre was at Briftol. In
the regifter of the Diocefe of Wells,
however, there are two perfons of the
name of Thomas Rowley, mentioned as
admitted into Holy Orders, one of whom
might be the author of the poems.*. In
anfwer to the objection, why thefe manufcripts remained fo long unknown to the
world, Mr. Bryant fays, "We may not
be able to account any more for thefe manufcripts being fo long neglected, than for
thofe of Hefychius, Phœdrus, and Velle-
ius

* Mr. Bryant's Obf. p. 535, 543 544.

ius Paterculus having been in the same fituation,*:" and with refpect to the fecreting of the-originals by Chatterton, it is deemed a fufficient reply, that he might conceive very highly of their value, and therefore did not wifh to part with them, or he might be apprehenfive that they would be taken from him; and at laft, in his indignation againft the world, he probably deftroyed all of them that remained at the time when he determined upon putting an end to his exiftence.

VII. The conceffions of the adverfaries ought not to pafs unnoticed on this occafion. Mr. Warton admits, "that fome poems written by Rowley might have been preferved in Canynge's cheft; but if there were any, they were fo enlarged and improved by Chatterton, as to become entirely new compofitions †;" and in a fub-

P. 3   fequent

* Ibid, 499.
† Hiftory of Englifh Poetry.

fequent, publication, fays, " I will not
deny that Chatterton might difcover
parchments of humble profe, containing
local memoirs and authentic deeds, illuf-
trating the hiftory of Briftol. He might
have difcovered biographical diaries, or
other notices of the lives of Canynge,
Ifcham, and Gorges." Thefe conceffions
at leaft imply fomething of a doubt on the
mind of the Laureat, concerning the exiftence of fome important manufcripts,
and feem of fome confideration in the
fcale of controverfy.

Internal Evidence in favour of the authen-
ticity of Rowley's Poems.

I. The internal evidence (which we
may call pofitive) on this fide of the queftion is not very extenfive, and the bulk
of it confifts in negative arguments, or a
refutation of the adverfaries' objections.
The moft material proof is derived from

the

the ALLUSIONS TO FACTS and CUSTOMS, of which there is not much probability, that Chatterton could have a competent knowledge. Thus, if the "Dethe of Sir Charles Bawdin" be fuppofed, as Mr. Tyrwhitt himfelf thinks probable, to refer to the execution of Sir Baldwin of Fulford, the fact meets confirmation in all its circumftances, from a fragment publifhed by Hearne, and alfo from a parliamentary roll of the eighth of Edward IV; neither which there is the leaft probability that Chatterton ever faw*. Thus the names which occur in the Battle of Haftings, may almoft all be authenticated from the old hiftorians; but they are fcattered in fuch a variety of books, that they could not be extracted without infinite labour, and feveral of the books were in all probability not acceffible by Chatterton.

P 4   To

* Obfervations on Rowley's poems, p. 14.

To this head we may refer many particulars concerning Canynge, &c. as related by Chatterton, such as his paying 3000 marks to the king, *pro pace sua habenda*, &c. which are confirmed in an extraordinary manner by W. of Worceſtre, whoſe book was not made public till 1778, and which it was therefore impoſſible Chatterton could ſee previous to the publication of his memoirs; ſuch is alſo the time of Canynge's entering into Holy Orders, which is confirmed by the Epiſcopal regiſter of Worceſter; and the anecdote of the ſteeple of Redcliffe church being burnt down by lightning in 1446. Of a ſimiliar kind is a circumſtance in the the orthography of the name *Feſcampe*, (which is the right orthography,) while Holingſhead, the only author acceſſible to Chatterton, has it *Fliſchampe*. The name of Robert Conſul alſo, whom Rowley repreſents as having repaired the caſtle of Briſtol,

Briſtol, occurs in Leland, as the proprietor of that Caſtle *.

II. With regard to the STYLE, COM-
POSITION, and SENTIMENT. If the
poems appear ſuperior to the efforts of the
firſt ſcholars at the revival of letters;
what are they, when conſidered as the
productions of an uneducated charity boy,
not quite ſeventeen? Thoſe alſo who think
that Chatterton could not reduce his genius
to the ſtandard of the age of Rowley,
ſhould, perhaps, rather wonder why he
could never raiſe his own avowed productions to an equal degree of excellence †.
The poems attributed to Rowley, if his,
are as much the work of his infantine
years, as his own miſcellaneous poems;
                                    indeed,

* See Bryant's Obſervations, p. 314, 326, 343, &c.

† The moſt eſſential difference that ſtrikes me between
the poems of Rowley and Chatterton is, that the former
are always built upon ſome conſiſtent intereſting plot, and
are more *uniformly* excellent in the execution; the latter are
irregular ſallies upon ill-ſelected or trifling ſubjects.

indeed; many of the latter were composed
some time after moft of Rowley's were
exhibited to the world; that they fhould
be inferior in every excellence of poetry,
is therefore a myftery not eafy to be accounted for. Againft the general propofi-
tion, that poetry like other arts is progref-
five, and never arrived to perfection in an
early age, it has been judicioufly urged, that
" Genius is peculiar neither to *age* nor
country," but that we have an example
of one man (Homer), who in the very
infancy of all arts, without guide or pre-
curfor, " gave to the world a work, which
has been the admiration and model of all
fucceeding poets †." And though it be
admitted, that Rowley's poems are per-
vaded by an uniform ftrain of excellence
and tafte, which does not appear in the
other works of his age now extant, yet
when

---

† Matthias's Effay, p. 98.

when we compare any composition with another of the same or of any prior age, the difference subsisting, will frequently be found not to depend upon *time*, but upon the situation, genius, and judgment of the respective authors †.

III. As to METRE, it is said, that in all languages the modes and measures of verse were originally invented and adopted from accidental circumstances, and agreeably to the taste of different authors; and that very early in the English poetry, a great variety of measures are known to have prevailed, such is the octave stanza, which is not many removes from the usual stanza of Rowley, the seven lined stanza, or Rithm Royal, and that of ten lines used by Chaucer in one of his smaller poems. The argument founded on the smoothness of the verse, is attempted to be overturned by Mr. Bryant;

* Matthias's Essay, p. 72. †

Bryant, who has produced extracts from poems still older than the age of Rowley, which are deficient neither in harmony nor cadence *.

IV. The objection founded on the ancient LANGUAGE of Rowley, is answered by supposing that his language was probably provincial †. Several of the words objected to as of Chatterton's coining, have by more profound researches been traced in ancient writers. Many words in Rowley's poems cannot be found in those dictionaries and glossaries, to which Chatterton had access ‡, and Chatterton's mistakes in transcribing and explaining the old language of Rowley, have already been instanced.

V. Many of the pretended IMITA-TIONS of THE MODERN poets to be found

---

* Observations, p. 425, &c. 552.
† Ibid, p, 1, to 25.
‡ Matthias's Essay, p. 77.

found in Rowley, are objected to upon good grounds, as being ideas obvious to Rowley or any man; and as to the others, why may we not suppose them, " insertions of Chatterton, either to please his own ear, or to restore some parts which were lost, or in places where the words were difficult to be decypered*?" This argument acquires great weight, when the temper and genius of Chatterton is considered, and when it is recollected that all parties agree in the probability of many interpolations being made by him; and if this argument be admitted, it will in a great measure account for the modern phrasology which so frequently occurs in these poems.

In rejoinder to these arguments, a few facts have been stated by those who support

port

* Matthias's Essay, p. 105.

port the title of Chatterton. 1ft. That no writings or cheſt depoſited in Redcliffe church are mentioned in Mr. Canynge's will, which has been carefully inſpected, nor any books except two, called "Liggers cum integra legenda," which he leaves to be uſed occaſionally in the choir by the two chaplains eſtabliſhed by him *. 2d. To account for Chatterton's extenſive acquaintance with old books out of the common line of reading, it is alledged that the old library at Briſtol was, during his life time, of univerſal acceſs, and Chatterton was actually introduced to it by the Rev. Mr. Catcott †. 3d. Chatterton's account of Canynge, &c. as far as it is countenanced by William of Worceſtre, (that is, as far as reſpects his taking orders and paying a fine to the king) may be found in the epitaph on Maſter Canynge, ſtill remaining to be read by every perſon, both in

Latin

---

* Tywrhitt's Vindication, p. 117.
† Warton's Inquiry, p. 111.

Latin and English, in Redcliffe church,
which indeed appears to be the authority,
that William of Worcestre himself has
followed. Chatterton's account also of
Redcliffe steeple, is to be found at the
bottom of a print of that church, published in 1746, by one John Halfpenny,
" in which was recounted the ruin of the
steeple in 1446, by a tempest and fire *."
4th. As to the old vellum or parchment
on which Chatterton transcribed his fragments, it is observed, that " at the bottom of each sheet of old deeds, (of which
there were many in the Bristol chest) there
is usually a blank space of about four or
five inches in breadth;" and this exactly agrees with the shape and size of the
largest fragment which he has exhibited,
viz. Eight and a half inches long, and
four and a half broad † .

* Tywrhitt's Vindication, p. 113, 212.
† Cursory Observations, p. 29.

THUS

THUS I have exhibited as faithfully as
I was able, an abſtract of the arguments
on both ſides of this curious literary queſtion. To the examination I ſat down with
a ſceptical mind; nor can I recollect being influenced during the progreſs of the
inquiry in a ſingle inſtance, by the authority of names, by the force of ridicule,
or the partialities of friendſhip. Some
remarks, I believe, I may have added,
which are not to be found in other books;
in this, however, I am not conſcious of
having favoured one party more than
the other, but eſteemed it a part of my
duty to ſtate the obſervations as they roſe
in my mind from a conſideration of the
facts. I ſhall not intrude upon my readers any verdict of my own concerning
the iſſue of the controverſy; ſince my
only intention was to enable them, from a
view of the arguments, to form their own
concluſions; leaving them ſtill open to
the

the impreſſion of any additional or more ſatisfactory evidence that may hereafter ariſe. | I cannot, however, lay aſide my pen without one general reflection. It is impoſſible to peruſe the ſtate of this controverſy, without ſmiling at the folly and vanity of poſthumous fame. The author, of theſe poems, whoever he was, certainly never flattered himſelf with the expectation that they would ever excite half the curioſity, or half the admiration which they have excited in the literary world. If they really be the productions of Rowley, one of the firſt, both in order and in merit of our Engliſh poets, is defrauded of more than half his reputation; if they be the works of Chatterton, they neither ſerved to raiſe him in the opinion of his intimate acquaintance and friends, nor to procure for him the comforts or even the neceſſaries of life. He has deſcended to his grave with a dubious cha-

Q   racter;

racter; and the only praise which can be accorded him by the warmeſt of his admirers, is that of an elegant and ingenious impoſtor.

For the ſatisfaction of thoſe readers, who may wiſh to review the whole controverſy at large, and for the information of poſterity, I ſubjoin the moſt accurate liſt I have been able to procure of all the publications which have appeared on both ſides.

A Liſt of the various Publications upon the Subject of ROWLEY's POEMS, *for* and *againſt* their *Authenticity*.

EDITIONS OF ROWLEY.

POEMS, ſuppoſed to have been written at Briſtol by Thomas Rowley, and others, in the Fifteenth Century; the greateſt Part now firſt publiſhed from the moſt authentic Copies, with an engraved Specimen of one of the MS. To which are added, a Preface, an Introductory Account of the ſeveral Pieces, and a Gloſſary. Ed. 8vo. 1777.

N. B. This Edition has been reprinted.

Ditto: with a Commentary, in which the Antiquity of them is conſidered and defended, by Jeremiah Milles, D. D. Dean of Exeter. Ed. 4to. 1782.

THE

THE EIGHTH Section of Mr. Warton's Second Volume of the History of English Poetry, with the Notes to it.

REMARKS on the Eighth Section of Mr. Warton's Second Volume of the History of English Poetry.

Payne, Mews-Gate.

TWO Letters by the Hon. Mr. Horace Walpole; printed at Strawberry-hill.—Reprinted, (by his permission) in the Gentleman's Magazines for April, May, June, July, 1782.

APPENDIX, containing some Observations upon the Language of the Poems attributed to Rowley, tending to prove, that they were written not by any ancient Author, but entirely by Thomas Chatterton. *Payne, Mews-Gate.*

N.B. This Appendix is *now* generally annexed to the 8vo. Edition of Rowley's Poems.

OBSERVATIONS on the Poems attributed to Rowley, tending to prove, that they were really written by Him and other Ancient Authors. To which are added, Remarks on the Appendix of the Editor (of the 8vo. Ed). of Rowley's Poems. *Bathurst, Fleet-Street.*

OBSERVATIONS upon the Poems of Thomas Rowley; in which the Authenticity of those Poems is ascertained. By Jacob Bryant, Esq. *Payne, Mews-Gate, &c.*

CURSORY Observations on the Poems attributed to Thomas Rowley, a Priest in the fifteenth Century: with some Remarks on the Commentaries on these Poems, by the Reverend Dr. Jeremiah Milles, Dean of Exeter, and Jacob Bryant, Esq. *Nichols and Walter, Charing-cross.*

AN ENQUIRY into the Authenticity of the Poems attributed to Thomas Rowley, in which the Arguments of the

Q 2   Dean

Dean of Exeter and Mr. Bryant are examined. By Thomas Warton, Fellow of Trinity College, Oxford, and F. S. A. *Dodſley, Pall-Mall.*

STRICTURES upon a Pamphlet entitled, " Curſory Obſervations on the Poems attributed to Rowley, a Prieſt in the Fifteenth Century." With a Poſtſcript on Mr. Thomas Warton's Enquiry into the ſame Subjeƈt. By. E. B. Greene, Eſq. *Stockdale, Piccadilly.*

A VINDICATION of the APPENDIX to the Poems called Rowley's: In Reply to the Anſwers of the Dean of Exeter, Jacob Bryant Eſq. and a third anonymous Writer; with ſome further obſervations upon thoſe Poems, and an Examination of the Evidence which has been produced in Support of their Authenticity. By Thomas Tyrwhitt.
Payne, Mew's-Gate.

AN ESSAY on the Evidence, External and Internal, relating to the Poems attributed to Thomas Rowley and others, in the Fifteenth Century, containing a general View of the whole Controverſy. By Thomas James Mathias.
Becket, Pall Mall.

To which may be added various ſhorter Compoſitions on the Subjeƈt (too numerous to ſpecify) inſerted in the different monthly Magazines.

APPENDIX.

APPENDIX.

The following Poem was copied from a manuscript of CHATTERTON, *and the Editor believes has never before been presented to the Public.*

The ART of PUFFING,

By a BOOKSELLER's JOURNEYMAN.

VERS'D by experience in the subtle art,
The myst'ries of a title I impart :
Teach the young author how to please the town;
And make the heavy drug of rhime go down.
Since Curl, immortal, never dying name,
A double pica in the book of fame,
By various arts did various dunces prop,
And tickled every fancy to his shop :
Who can like Pottinger ensure a book ?
Who judges with the solid taste of Cooke ?
Villains exalted in the midway sky,
Shall live again, to drain your purses dry :
Nor yet unrivall'd they ; see Baldwin comes,
Rich in inventions, patents, cuts and hums :
The honorable Boswell writes, 'tis true,
What else can Paoli's supporter do ?

The

The trading wits endeavour to attain,
Like bookfellers, the world's firft idol—gain:
For this they puff the heavy Goldfmith's line,
And hail his fentiment tho' trite, divine;
For this, the patriotic bard complains,
And Bingley binds poor liberty in chains:
For this was every reader's faith deceiv'd,
And Edmund fwore what nobody believ'd:
For this the wits in clofe difguifes fight;
For this the varying politicians write;
For this each month new magazines are fold,
With dulnefs fill'd and tranfcripts of the old,
The Town and Country ftruck a lucky hit,
Was novel, fentimental, full of wit:
Apeing her walk, the fame fuccefs to find,
The Court and City hobbles far behind:
Sons of Apollo learn, merit's no more
Than a good frontifpiece to grace her door;
The author who invents a title well,
Will always find his cover'd dulnefs fell;
Flexney and every bookfeller will buy;—
Bound in neat calf, the work will never die.

VAMP.

July 22, 1770.

LETTERS

LETTERS

OF

THOMAS CHATTERTON.

LETTER I.

London, April 26, 1770.

Dear Mother,

HERE I am, safe, and in high spirits
—To give you a journal of my tour
would not be unnecessary. After riding
in the basket to Brislington, I mounted
the top of the coach, and rid easy; and
agreeably entertained with the conversation of a quaker *in dress,* but little so in
personals and behaviour. This laughing
friend, who is a carver, lamented his
having sent his tools to Worcester, as
otherwise he would have accompanied me

Q 4

to

to London. I left him at Bath; when, finding it rained pretty faſt, I entered an inſide paſſenger to Speenhamland, the half-way ſtage, paying ſeven ſhillings. 'Twas lucky I did ſo, for it ſnowed all night, and on Marlborough Downs the ſnow was near a foot high.

At ſeven in the morning I breakfaſted at Speenhamland, and then mounted the coach-box for the remainder of the day, which was a remarkable fine one. — Honeſt gee-ho complimented me with aſſuring me, that I ſat bolder and tighter than any perſon who ever rid with him. —Dined at Stroud moſt luxuriantly, with a young gentleman who had ſlept all the preceding night in the machine; and an old mercantile genius, whoſe ſchool-boy ſon had a great deal of wit, as the father thought, in remarking that Windſor was as old as *our Saviour's* time.

Got

Got into London about five o'clock in the evening—called upon Mr. Edmunds, Mr. Fell, Mr. Hamilton, and Mr. Dodf-ley. Great encouragement from them; all approved of my defign;—fhall foon be fettled.——Call upon Mr. Lambert; fhew him this, or tell him, if I deferve a recommendation, he would oblige me to give me one—if I do not, it will be beneath him to take notice of me. Seen all aunts, coufins—all well—and I am welcome. Mr. T. Wenfley is alive, and coming home.——Sifter, grandmother, &c. &c. &c. remember.—I remain,

Your dutiful fon,

T. Chatterton.

LETTER

LETTER II.

Shoreditch, London, May 6, 1770.

Dear Mother,

I am furprifed that no letter has been fent in anfwer to my laft. I am fettled, and in fuch a fettlement as I would defire. I get four guineas a month by one Magazine: fhall engage to write a Hiftory of England, and other pieces, which will more than double that fum. Occafional effays for the daily papers would more than fupport me. What a glorious profpect! Mr. Wilkes knew me by my writings fince I firft correfponded with the bookfellers here. I fhall vifit him next week, and by his intereft will infure Mrs. Ballance the Trinity-Houfe. He affirmed that what Mr. Fell had of mine could not be the writings of a youth; and expreffed a defire to know the author. By the means of another

bookfeller

bookſeller I ſhall be introduced to Townſhend and Sawbridge. I am quite familiar
at the Chapter Coffee-houſe, and know
all the geniuſes there. A character is
now unneceſſary; an author carries his
character in his pen. My ſiſter will improve herſelf in drawing. My grandmother is, I hope, well. Briſtol's mercenary walls were never deſtined to hold
me—there I was out of my element;
now, I am in it—London! Good God!
how ſuperior is London to that deſpica-
ble place Briſtol!—Here is none of your
little meanneſſes, none of your mercenary
ſecurities, which diſgrace that miſerable
hamlet.—Dreſs, which is in Briſtol an
eternal fund of ſcandal, is here only introduced as a ſubject of praiſe; if a man
dreſſes well, he has taſte; if careleſs, he
has his own reaſons for ſo doing, and is
prudent. Need I remind you of the
contraſt? The poverty of authors is a
common

common obfervation, but not always a true one. No author can be poor who underftands the arts of bookfellers—Without this neceffary knowledge, the greateft genius may ftarve; and, with it, the greateft dunce live in fplendor. This knowledge I have pretty well dipped into.—The Levant man of war, in which T. Wenfley went out, is at Portf-mouth; but no news from him yet.—I lodge in one of Mr. Walmfley's beft rooms. Let Mr. Cary copy the letters on the other fide, and give them to the per-fons for whom they are defigned, if not too much labour for him.

I remain, yours, &c.

T. Chatterton.

P. S. I have fome trifling prefents for my mother, fifter Thorne, &c.

Sunday morning,

For

For Mr. T. CARY.

I have sent you a task. I hope no unpleasing one. Tell all your acquaintance for the future to read the Freeholder's Magazine. When you have any thing for publication, send it to me, and it shall most certainly appear in some periodical compilation. Your last piece was, by the ignorance of a corrector, jumbled under the considerations in the acknowledgements. But I rescued it, and insisted on its appearance.

Your friend,

T. C.

Direct for me, to be left at the Chapter Coffee-house, Pater-noster-row.

Mr. HENRY KATOR.

If you have not forgot Lady Betty, any Complaint, Rebus, or Enigma, on the dear charmer, directed for me, to be left at

the

the Chapter. Coffee-houfe, Pater-nofter-row—fhall find a place in fome Magazine, or other; as I am engaged in many.

Your friend,

T. Chatterton.

Mr. WILLIAM SMITH.

When you have any poetry for publication, fend it to me, to be left at the Chapter Coffee-houfe, Pater-nofter-row, and it fhall moft certainly appear.

Your friend,

T. C.

Mrs. BAKER.

The fooner I fee you the better—fend me as foon as poffible Rymfdyk's addrefs.

(Mr. Cary will leave this at Mr. Flower's, Small-ftreet.)

Mr. MASON.

Give me a fhort profe defcription of the fituation of Nafh—and the poetic addition

fhall

ſhall appear in ſome Magazine. Send me alſo whatever you would have publiſhed, and direct for me, to be left at the Chapter Coffee-houſe, Pater-noſter-row.

Your friend,

T. Chatterton.

Mr. MAT. MEASE.

Begging Mr. Meaſe's pardon for making public uſe of his name lately—I hope he will remember me, and tell all his acquaintance to read the Freeholder's Magazine for the future.

T. Chatterton.

TELL——

Mr. Thaire	Mr. Rudhall	Mr. Ward
Mr. Gaſter	Mr. Thomas	Mr. Kalo
Mr. A. Broughton	Mr. Carty	Mr. Smith
Mr. J. Broughton	Mr. Hanmor	&c. &c.
Mr. Williams	Mr. Vaughan	

to read the Freeholder's Magazine.

LETTER

LETTER III.

King's Bench, for the present, May 14, 1770.

Dear Madam,

Don't be furprized at the name of the place. I am not here as a prifoner. Matters go on fwimmingly: Mr. Fell having offended certain perfons, they have fet his creditors upon him, and he is fafe in the King's Bench. I have been bettered by this accident : His fuccellors in the Freeholder's Magazine, knowing nothing of the matter, will be glad to engage me, on my own terms. Mr. Edmunds has been tried before the Houfe of Lords, fentenced to pay a fine, and thrown into Newgate. His misfortunes will be to me of no little fervice. Laft week, being in the pit of Drury Lane, Theatre, I contracted an immediate acquaintance (which you know is no hard tafk to me) with a young gentle-

man

man in Cheapſide; partner in a muſic ſhop, the greateſt in the city. Hearing I could write, he deſired me to write a few ſongs for him: this I did the ſame night, and conveyed them to him the next morning. Theſe he ſhewed to a Doctor in Muſic, and I am invited to treat with this Doctor, on the footing of a compoſer, for Ranelagh and the Gardens. *Bravo, hey boys, up we go!* — Beſides the advantage of viſiting theſe expenſive and polite places gratis; my vanity will be fed with the ſight of my name in copper-plate, and my ſiſter will receive a bundle of printed ſongs, the words by her brother. Theſe are not all my acquiſitions: a gentleman who knows me at the Chapter, as an author, would have introduced me as a-companion to the young Duke of Northumberland, in his intended general tour. But, alas! I ſpeak no tongue but my own! — But to return once more to a place I am

R ſickened

fickened to write of, Briftol. Though, as an apprentice, none had greater liberties, yet the thoughts of fervitude killed me: now I have that for my labour, I always reckoned the firft of my pleafures, and have ftill, my liberty. As to the clearance, I am ever ready to give it; but really I underftand fo little of the law, that I believe Mr. Lambert muft draw it. Mrs. L. brought what you mention. Mrs. Hughes is as well as age will permit her to be, and my coufin does very well.

I will get fome patterns worth your acceptance; and wifh you and my fifter would improve yourfelves in drawing, as it is here a valuable and never-failing acquifition.——My box fhall be attended to; I hope my books are in it—if not, fend them; and particularly Catcott's Hutchinfonian jargon on the Deluge, and the M.S. Gloffary, compofed of one fmall book, annexed to a larger.——My fifter

fifter will remember me to Mifs Sandford.
I have not quite forgot her; though there
are fo many pretty milleners, &c. that
I have almoſt forgot myſelf.——Carty
will think on me: upon inquiry, I find
his trade dwindled into nothing here.
A man may very nobly ſtarve by it; but
he muſt have luck indeed, who can live
by it.——Mifs Rumſey, if ſhe comes to
London, would do well, as an old acquaintance, to ſend me her addreſs.——
London is not Briſtol—We may patrole
the town for a day, without raiſing one
whiſper, or nod of ſcandal.—If ſhe re-
fuſes, the curſe of all antiquated virgins
light on her: may ſhe be refuſed, when
ſhe ſhall requeſt! Mifs Rumſey will tell
Mifs Baker, and Mifs Baker will tell Mifs
Porter, that Mifs Porter's favoured humble ſervant, though but a *young* man, is a
very old lover; and in the eight-and-
fiftieth year of his age: but that, as Lap-

pet

pet says, is the flower of a man's days;
and when a lady can't get a young hufband, she muft put up with an old bed-
fellow. I left Mifs Singer, I am forry
to fay it, in a very bad way; that is, in a
way to be married.——But mum—Afk
Mifs Suky Webb the reft; if she knows,
she'll tell ye.—I beg her pardon for re-
vealing the fecret; but when the knot is
faftened, she shall know how I came by
it.—Mifs Thatcher may depend upon it,
that, if I am not in love with her, I am
in love with nobody elfe: I hope she is
well; and if that whining, fighing, dying pulpit-fop, Lewis, has not finifhed
his languifhing lectures, I hope she will
fee her amorofo next Sunday.—If Mifs
Love has no objection to having a crambo
fong on her name publifhed, it shall be
done.—Begging pardon of Mifs Cotton
for whatever has happened to offend her,
I can affure her it has happened without

m y

my confent: I did not give her this af-
furance when in Briftol, left it fhould
feem like an attempt to avoid the anger
of her *furious* brother. Inquire, when
you can, how Mifs Broughton received
her billet. Let my fifter fend me a journal of all the tranfactions of the females
within the circle of your acquaintance.
Let Mifs Watkins know, that the letter
fhe made herfelf ridiculous by, was never
intended for her; but another young lady
in the neighbourhood, of the fame name.
I promifed, before my departure, to write
to fome hundreds, I believe; but, what
with writing for publications, and going
to places of public diverfion, which is
as abfolutely neceffary to me as food, I
find but little time to write to you. As
to Mr. Barrett, Mr. Catcott, Mr. Bur-
gum, &c. &c. they rate literary lumber
fo low, that I believe an author, in their
eftimation, muft be poor indeed! But

here

here matters are otherwise; had Rowley
been a Londoner, inſtead of a Briſtowyan,
I could have lived by copying his works.
——In my humble opinion, I am under
very few obligations to any perſons in
Briſtol: one, indeed, has obliged me; but,
as moſt do, in a manner which makes his
obligation no obligation.—My youthful
acquaintances will not take it in dudgeon,
that I do not write oftener to them, than
I believe I ſhall: but, as I had the happy
art of pleaſing in converſation, my company was often liked, where I did not
like: and to continue a correſpondence
under ſuch circumſtances, would be ridiculous. Let my ſiſter improve in copying,
muſic, drawing, and every thing which
requires genius: in Briſtol's mercantile
ſtyle thoſe things may be uſeleſs, if not
a detriment to her; but here they are
highly profitable.——Inform Mr. Rhiſe,
that nothing ſhall be wanting, on my
part,

part, in the bufinefs he was fo kind as to employ me in; fhould be glad of a line from him, to know whether he would engage in the marine department; or fpend the reft of his days, fafe, on dry ground.—Intended waiting on the Duke of Bedford relative to the Trinity-Houfe; but his Grace is dangeroufly ill. My grandmother, I hope, enjoys the ftate of health I left her in. I am Mifs Webb's humble fervant. Thorne fhall not be forgot, when I remit the fmall trifles to you. Notwithftanding Mrs. B's not being able to inform me of Mr. Garfed's addrefs, through the clofenefs of the pious Mr. Ewer, I luckily ftumbled upon it this morning.

I remain, &c. &c. &c. &c.

Monday Evening. Thomas Chatterton.

(Direct for me, at Mr. Walmfley's, at Shoreditch—only.)

R 4 LETTER

LETTER IV.

Tom's Coffee-house, London, May 30, 1770.

Dear Sister,

There is such a noise of business and politicks in the room, that my inaccuracy in writing here, is highly excusable. My present profession obliges me to frequent places of the best resort. To begin with, what every female conversation begins with, dress: I employ my money now in fitting myself fashionably, and getting into good company; this last article always brings me in interest. I have engaged to live with a gentleman, the brother of a Lord (a Scotch one indeed), who is going to advance pretty deeply into the bookselling branches: I shall have lodging and boarding, genteel and elegant, gratis: this article, in the quarter of the town he lives, with worse accommodations, would be 50l. per annum.

I shall

I shall have, likewise, no inconsiderable
premium; and assure yourself every month
shall end to your advantage: I will send
you two silks this summer; and expect,
in answer to this, what colours you prefer. My mother shall not be forgotten.
My employment will be writing a voluminous History of London, to appear in
numbers the beginning of the next winter. As this will not, like writing political essays, oblige me to go to the coffee-
house, I shall be able to serve you the
more by it: but it will necessitate me to
go to Oxford, Cambridge, Lincoln, Coventry, and every collegiate church near;
not at all disagreeable journeys, and not
to me expensive. The Manuscript Glossary, I mentioned in my last, must not
be omitted. If money flowed as fast
upon me as honours, I would give you a
portion of 5000 l. You have, doubtless,
heard of the Lord Mayor's remonstrating

and

and addreffing the King: but it will be a piece of news, to inform you that I have been with the Lord Mayor on the occafion. Having addreffed an effay to his Lordfhip, it was very well received; perhaps better than it deferved; and I waited on his Lordfhip, to have his approbation, to addrefs a fecond letter to him, on the fubject of the remonftrance, and its reception. His Lordfhip received me as politely as a citizen could; and warmly invited me to call on him again. The reft is a fecret———But the devil of the matter is, there's no money to be got of this fide the queftion. Intereft is of the other fide. But he is a poor author, who cannot write on both fides. I believe I may be introduced (and, if I am not, I'll introduce myfelf) to a ruling power in the Court party. I might have a recommendation to Sir George Colebrook, an Eaft-India Director, as quali-

fied

fied for an office no ways defpicable; but
I fhall not take a ftep to the fea, whilft I
can continue on land. I went yefterday
to Woolwich, to fee Mr. Wenfley; he is
paid to-day. The artillery is no unplea-
fing fight, if we bar reflection, and do
not confider how much mifchief it may
do. Greenwich Hofpital and St. Paul's
Cathedral are the only ftructures which
could reconcile me to any thing out of
the Gothic. Mr. Carty will hear from
me foon: multiplicity of literary bufinefs muft be my excufe.—I condole with
him, and my dear Mifs Sandford, in the
misfortune of Mrs. Carty: my phyfical
advice is, to leech her temples plenti-
fully; keep her very low in diet; as
much in the dark as poffible. Nor is
this laft prefcription the whim of an old
woman: whatever hurts the eyes, affects
the brain; and the particles of light,

when

when the fun is in the fummer figns, are
highly prejudicial to the eyes; and it is
from this fympathetic effect, that the
head-ach is general in fummer. But,
above all, talk to her but little, and never contradict her in any thing. This
may be of fervice. I hope it will. Did
a paragraph appear in your paper of Saturday laft, mentioning the inhabitants of
London's having opened another view of
St. Paul's; and advifing the corporation,
or veftry of Redclift, to procure a more
compleat view of Redclift church? My
compliments to Mifs Thatcher: if I am
in love, I am; though the devil take me,
if I can tell with whom it is. I believe
I may addrefs her in the words of Scripture, which no doubt fhe reveres; "If
you had not ploughed with my heifer."
(or bullock rather), if you had not found
out my riddle." Humbly thanking Mifs

Rumfey

Rumſey for her complimentary expreſſion, I cannot think it ſatisfactory. Does ſhe, or does ſhe not, intend coming to London? Mrs. O'Coffin has not yet got a place; but there is not the leaſt doubt but ſhe will in a little time.

Eſſay-writing has this advantage, you are ſure of conſtant pay; and when you have once wrote a piece which makes the author enquired after, you may bring the bookſellers to your own terms. Eſſays on the patriotic ſide fetch no more than what the copy is ſold for. As the patriots themſelves are ſearching for a place, they have no gratuities to ſpare. So ſays one of the beggars, in a temporary alteration of mine, in the Jovial Crew:

A patriot was my occupation,
　It got me a name but no pelf:
Till, ſtarv'd for the good of the nation,
　I begg'd for the good of myſelf.
　　　　　　Fal, lal, &c.

I told

I told them; if 'twas not for me,
　　Their freedoms would all go to pot;
　I promis'd to set them all free,
　　But never a farthing I got:
　　　　　　Fal, lal, &c.

—On the other hand, unpopular essays
will not even be accepted; and you must
pay to have them printed: but then you
seldom lose by it. Courtiers are so sen-
sible of their deficiency in merit, that
they generally reward all who know how,
to daub them with an appearance of it.
To return to private affairs —— Friend
Slude may depend upon my endeavouring
to find the publications you mention.
They publish the Gospel Magazine here.
For a whim I write in it. I believe there
are not any sent to Bristol; they are hardly worth the carriage—methodistical, and
unmeaning. With the usual ceremonies
to my mother, and grandmother; and sincerely, without ceremony, wishing them
　　　　　　　　　　　　　　　both

both happy; when it is in my power to
make them fo, they fhall be fo; and with
my kind remembrance to Mifs Webb, and
Mifs Thorne; I remain, as I ever was,

Yours, &c. to the end of the chapter,

Thomas Chatterton.

P. S. I am this minute pierced through
the heart by the black eye of a young
lady, driving along in a Hackney-coach.
——I am quite in love: if my love lafts
till that time, you fhall hear of it in my
next.

LETTER V.

June 19, 1770.

Dear Sifter,

I have an horrid cold——The relation
of the manner of my catching it may
give you more pleafure than the circumftance itfelf. As I wrote very late Sunday
night

night (or rather very early Monday morning), I thought to have gone to bed pretty foon laft night: when, being half undreffed, I heard a very doleful voice, finging Mifs Hill's favorite bedlamite fong. The hum-drum of the voice fo ftruck me, that though I was obliged to liften a long while before I could hear the words, I found the fimilitude in the found. After hearing her with pleafure drawl for above half an hour, fhe jumped into a brifker tune, and hobbled out the ever-famous fong, in which poor Jack Fowler was to have been fatirized.——

" I put my hand into a bufh : I prick'd
" my finger to the bone : I faw a fhip
" failing along : I thought the fweeteft
" flowers to find:" and other pretty flowery expreffions, were twanged with no inharmonious bray.——I now ran to the window, and threw up the fafh; refolved to be fatisfied, whether or no it

was

was the identical Mifs Hill, *in propria
perfona*.——But, alas! it was a perfon
whofe twang is very well known, when
fhe is awake, but who had drank fo much
royal bob (the gingerbread-baker for that,
you know), that fhe was now finging herfelf afleep. This fomnifying liquor had
made her voice fo like the fweet echo of
Mifs Hill's, that if I had not confidered
that fhe could not fee her way up to
London, I fhould abfolutely have imagined it hers ———There was a fellow and
a girl in one corner, more bufy in at-
tending to their own affairs, than the
melody.

*This part of the letter, for fome lines,
is not legible.*

. . . . . . the morning) from Marybone
gardens; I faw the fellow in the cage at
the watch-houfe, in the parifh of St.
Giles; and the nymph is an inhabitant of
one of Cupid's inns of Court.——There
was one fimilitude it would be injuftice

S

to let flip. A drunken fifhman, who fells
foufe mackarel, and other delicious dain-
ties, to the eternal detriment of all two-
penny ordinaries; as his beft commodity,
his falmon, goes off at three halfpence
the piece: this itinerant merchant, this
moveable fifh-ftall, having likewife had
his dofe of bob-royal; ftood ftill for a
while; and then joined chorus, in a tone
which would have laid half a dozen law-
yers, pleading for their fees, faft afleep:
this naturally reminded me of Mr. Hay-
thorne's fong of

"Says Plato, who oy oy oy fhould man be vain?"

However, my entertainment, though
fweet enough in itfelf has a difh of four
fauce ferved up in it; for I have a moft
horrible wheezing in the throat: but I
don't repent that I have this cold; for
there are fo many noftrums here, that 'tis
worth a man's while to get a diftemper,
he can be cured fo cheap.

June 29th, 1770.

My

My cold is over and gone. If the above did not recall to your mind some scenes of laughter, you have lost your ideas of rifibility.

———————

LETTER VI.*

Dear Mother,

I fend you in the box—fix cups and faucers with two bafons, for my fifter—If a china tea pot and cream pot, is in your opinion, neceffary, I will fend them, but I am informed they are unfafhionable, and that the red china, which you are provided with, is more in ufe———a cargo of patterns, for yourfelf, with a fnuff box, right French and very curious in my opinion.

S 2   Two

* Chatterton had probably changed his lodging a little before he wrote this letter. It is a remarkable paffage, where he fays, he wifhes fhe had fent him up his red pocket book, "as 'tis very material." "More. graver," in the 13th line, confirms Mr. Bryant's opinion, p. 481, "that he was not well grounded in the firft principles of Grammar."

Two fans—the silver one, is more graver than the other, which would fuit my fifter beft——But that I leave to you both.

Some Britifh herb fnuff, in the box; be careful how you open it—(This I omit left it injure the other matters)

Some Britifh herb tobacco for my grand-mother, fome trifles for Thorne. Be af-fured whenever I have the power, my will won't be wanting to teftify, that I re-member you——

Yours,

July 8, 1770. T. Chatterton.

N. B.—I fhall foreftall your intended journey, and pop down upon you at Chriftmas——

I could have wifhed, you had fent my red pocket book, as 'tis very material

I bought two very curious twifted pipes for my grandmother; but both breaking; I was afraid to buy others left they fhould break

break in the box; and being loose, injure the china.—Have you heard any thing further of the clearance.——

Direct for me at Mrs. Angels', Sack-maker, Brooke Street, Holborn.

"Mrs. Chatterton."

———

LETTER VII.

Dear Sister,

I have sent you some china and a fan. You have your choice of two. I am surprised that you chose purple and gold. I went into the shop to buy it: but it is the most disagreeable colour I ever saw— dead, lifeless, and inelegant. Purple and pink, or lemon and pink, are more genteel and lively. Your answer in this affair will oblige me. Be assured, that I shall ever make your wants, my wants; and stretch to the utmost to serve you. Remember me to Miss Sandford, Miss Rumfey, Miss Singer, &c. &c. &c.

As

As to the songs, I have waited this week for them, and have not had time to copy one perfectly: when the season's over, you will have 'em all in print. I had pieces last month in the following Magazines:

Gospel Magazine,
Town and Country, viz.
Maria Friendless.
False Step.
Hunter of Oddities,
To Miss Bush, &c.

Court and City. London. Political Register, &c. &c.

The Christian Magazine, as they are not to be had perfect, are not worth buying——I remain,

Yours,

T. Chatterton.

July 11, 1770.

LET-

LETTER VIII.

I am now about an Oratorio, which, when finished, will purchase you a gown. You may be certain of seeing me before the 1ſt of January, 1771.—The clearance is immaterial.—My mother may expect more patterns.—Almoſt all the next Town and Country Magazine is mine. I have an univerſal acquaintance:—my company is courted every where; and, could I humble myſelf to go into a compter, could have had twenty places before now;—but I muſt be among the great; ſtate matters ſuit me better than commercial. The ladies are not out of my acquaintance. I have a deal of buſineſs now, and muſt therefore bid you adieu. You will have a longer letter from me ſoon——and more to the purpoſe.

Yours,

T. C.

20th July, 1770.

F I N I S.

THE RESIGNATION.

BY THOS. CHATTERTON.

O GOD! whose thunders shaking
   the sky,
Whose eye this atom globe sur-
   veys,
To thee, my only rock, I fly;
   Thy mercy in thy justice praise.
The mystic mazes of thy will,
   The shadows of celestial night.
Are past the pow'rs of human skill;
   But what the Eternal acts is
    right.

O teach me, in this trying hour,
   When anguish swells the dewy
    tear,
To still my sorrows, own thy
   pow'r,
   Thy goodness love, thy justice
    fear.

If in this bosom aught but thee,
   Incroaching, sought a boundless
    sway,
Omniscience could the danger see,
   And mercy took the cause away.

Then why, my soul, dost thou
   complain?
   Why drooping seek the dark re-
    cess?
Shake off the melancholy chain,
   For God created all to bless.

But, ah! my breast is human still,
   The rising sigh, the falling tear,
My languid vitals feeble rill,
   The sickness of my soul declare.

But yet, with fortitude resign'd,
   I'll thank the inflictor of the
    blow;
Forbid the sigh, compose my mind,
   Nor let the gush of misery flow.
The gloomy mantle of the night,
   Which on my sinking spirit
    steals,
Will vanish at the morning light,
   Which God, my East, my Sun
    reveals.